Breaking the Cycle of
Slavery to Sin

Breaking the Cycle of Slavery to Sin

by
Gordon Magee
of Christ Light Ministries

cᑭ
Aventine Press

Published by Aventine Press
1202 Donax Ave Suite 12
Imperial Beach, CA 91932, USA
www.aventinepress.com

ISBN: 1-59330-163-4
Printed in the United States of America

Dedication

I dedicate this book to Jesus Christ, my Lord and Savior, the one who reconciled me to God the Father and has set me free from slavery to Sin. As promised in the Bible, He has been with me always. He is a constant source of encouragement and correction. He has provided His word as a lamp for my feet and a light for my path and has given me of His Spirit to lead me in this life. Thank you Jesus!

I also want to dedicate this book to my wife Petra, whom God has used in marvelous ways in my life. Much of what I learned about love and a heart of compassion for others I learned from her. It has been largely through her patience and love for me, through her ability to stand her ground, that I learned to keep focused on growing in my own maturity. I love you Petra!

For my children, I leave this to you as a legacy, as a record of and reference to many of the things that God has taught me. May it help you to know me better and also shed light on God's will for your lives. You are all very special and precious to me.

And for every person who is struggling in this life. I pray God's encouragement on to you and in to you. In the Lord there is hope, read on. You can be free, first on the inside with the Lord and then on the outside among your fellow man.

Table of Contents

Part 3: Living a Life of Freedom.
(Living in Partnership with God.)

Introduction:
Don't skip the Introduction!
(Help for everyone who wants to live free.)

This book was originally written for men and women alike who are now in prison or whose slavery to sin is likely to land them back in prison. One of the ministries that God has put me into is cell-to-cell visitation. It is through my time spent talking to and listening to prisoners that God has directed me to write this book with prisoners in mind. At the same time, what the prisoner needs is the same as what every person needs. If you are lost in this world, if you are trapped in a cycle of recurring slavery to sin that keeps messing up your life, if you just haven't found how to follow the Lord in doing what is right on a regular basis, these words were written for you.

I have been a Christian for more than twenty-six years. I started out as a mess, addicted to Heroin and enslaved to all manner of evil habits and emotional problems. The Lord has led me to salvation and then He has led me through both cleaning up my life and learning to live for Him. He has involved me in many ministries from preaching and teaching the Bible to short term mission trips, Gospel outreaches, and various kinds of service for His kingdom. The things I have written in this book are things which God has worked in me over the years and which I have actually lived. Within these chapters I will give you some of my own testimony. But...I want you to understand from the start that these things are not important because of me or because I say so. Rather they are truths based on the testimony of God's word the Bible and what He has taught and done in me through His word and His Holy Spirit over these years of following Him.

Right up front, this book will bring you face to face with your need to do business with God's Son Jesus Christ. These words are intended to cut right to the heart of the matter. Part one is all about our need for salvation. If you are lost and your soul is hungry for the truth about yourself and God or if you are just unsure about that prayer for salvation you made some time ago then this is for you. Part two explores the many areas in which, even after salvation, we can be in slavery to sin and how God can help you work through and come to freedom from each one of them. His plan for us is that we all grow up into the fullness of His Son Jesus Christ. This is where we work with God to break the hold that repeating or difficult sin has on us. Part three is about living in the freedom of partnership with God. Wherever you go in this world, whether you have to work hard for every penny, or whether you always have plenty, whether your family is around you, or you end up living alone, even through something as hard as a long prison sentence, you will only find freedom and peace as you learn to walk daily with God.

This book is not going to spend time trying to prove that God exists or that the Bible is His word to man. If you have problems with either of these then I challenge you to the bravery that asks God to make Himself known to you and to show you if the Bible is His word. That bravery includes you doing your part of reading the Bible and taking your questions to God each day in prayer. I suggest you start with the New Testament if you are not familiar with the Bible. All quotations in this book are taken from the New King James Version of the Bible (NKJV). It is a standard, word for word translation, which means that there is an English word for every one of the original language words instead of a translator's opinion on what the Bible passages mean. You can still find the passages, which I have used, in any other translation by following the reference given. The end of this introduction will quote Acts 4:12 which you can find in any Bible by looking up the book of Acts in the table of contents, then the 4th chapter and 12th verse.

Whatever other practices or religions you have been into you will have to be the judge of them. But God has made a path of freedom from slavery to sin through Jesus and here it is. I don't mean any arrogance but as Acts 4:12 states: "there is no other name under heaven given among men by which we must be saved."

Our Focus Verse for the three Parts of this Book is John 14:6

"Jesus said to him, 'I am the way, the truth, and the life. No one comes to the Father except through Me.'"

Part One

Freedom from Eternal Punishment,

Jesus is the Way!

Chapter One

Lost in this World.

So many of us are just plain lost in this world. If we will admit it this world is a scary place to be. We have not found the way or even any way that seems to really work for us. Often we have been discouraged in life by the people we know or the circumstances we find ourselves in. But because we have a basic God given need to fit in we all chose a place for ourselves. Some of us have even chosen prison, bad as it is, as the only place where we seem to feel 'at home' or like we fit in. So we keep doing things that get us back there. Think about yourself for a while, what have you chosen? It could be a place or it could be the way you present yourself to people, (tough person, angry person, weak person). All of these things become places for lost people to hide.

What is it about being lost? The Bible says that even those who follow Jesus now were lost once, "having no hope and without God in the world," Ephesians 2:12. Over thousands of years man has created many religions. Some of them seem pretty good. Some of them are obviously evil. All of them are an attempt to either know God or to relate to him in some way. Even Christianity can become no more than a dead religion if it follows the traditions of men rather than God. One way or another our lost-ness calls us to either seek God or settle for a life that works as best we know how. Why is this and what is our basic problem?

Our most basic problem is that all of us are sinners. The Bible story of Adam and Eve shows that they made a choice to join those who disobey God. By their selfish choice of disobedience toward God they joined the camp of Satan whose very nature is selfishness. By this the nature of sin entered all mankind and you and I have inherited a sinful, self-centered nature that is at odds with following God. We want to do what we want to do when we want to do it. Even our heart justifies us in much wrong doing putting the blame for our actions and choices on others or deciding that we can do what we want now because we have balanced it with enough good or by refusing to look at our wrong because we are angry. On top of this sinful nature in us we have all added many sins, which we have committed in this lifetime. Some of these sins are horribly evil and others are less but they are all an expression of our evil nature. In Romans 3:10-12 the word of God says that we are all equal in this before God, "There is none righteous, no, not one; There is none who understands; there is none who seeks after God. They have all turned aside; they have together become unprofitable; there is none who does good, no, not one".

What does this do to any relationship we should have with God? We would all like to think that we are going to heaven after we die. After all hasn't our life on earth been hard enough? Isn't God good rather than condemning? Others of us greatly fear death. We know we have done much evil and will probably be punished by God. The bottom line is that being sinful puts all of us under the same sentence of eternal punishment as the devil and his angels. This is taught throughout the Bible. Sin separates us from God. Isaiah 59:1-2 reads: "Behold, the LORD's hand is not shortened, That it cannot save; Nor His ear heavy, That it cannot hear. But your iniquities have separated you from your God; and your sins have hidden His face from you, So that He will not hear". In Matthew 25:41 Jesus speaks to those who died in their sins: "Depart from Me, you cursed, into the everlasting fire prepared for the devil and his angels". So sin puts separation between God and us, a sinful nature in particular puts us in the same camp as the devil and under condemnation of eternal punishment after this life.

Now I told you in the introduction that I would not try to prove to you that there is a God who not only created this world and universe but who also cares about you and me. I personally have discovered (or rather was discovered by) God. I have spent and am spending the time to get to know Him and I know that He not only cares about me but that He takes action because of that care. God both knows you and knows all about your sinful nature and the sins that you have committed. He created you intending that you would belong to His family. The very reason that you are reading this is because you know that everything is not right between you and God. God loves you and doesn't want you to remain lost and separated from Him through your sin. Whether you realize it or not, He has put in your heart a desire that draws you back to Him, that wants to be right with God.

Now I want you to think about this for a moment: how can we find the right way for our lives? Isn't God the one who would know? Therefore we have to be careful about what we accept from man. Man has many supposedly great thinkers and religions but if they don't agree with

God then they are not worth listening to. In John 8:32 Jesus said, "And you shall know the truth, and the truth shall make you free". If we are to be free then the truth we need is God's truth not man's opinions. If we are to find the way then the way we need is God's way not man's way. God Himself declares a difference between His thoughts His way and Man's thoughts Man's way in Isaiah 55:8-9, "'For My thoughts are not your thoughts, Nor are your ways My ways,' says the LORD. 'For as the heavens are higher than the earth, so are My ways higher than your ways, And My thoughts than your thoughts'".

At the birth of Christ the angel, who was sent to tell the shepherds, proclaimed "Do not be afraid, for behold, I bring you good tidings of great joy which will be to all people. For there is born to you this day in the city of David a Savior, who is Christ the Lord", Luke 2:10-11. God's answer to our need is to send us a Savior, one who saves. This one will not only show us the way but will be the way for us to follow, (Jesus is the way). Jesus is someone who can deal with the problem of our sin. Someone who can rescue us from the cycle of sin that seems to keep us in bondage. Someone who can really be our 'higher power' to trust in, depend on, and lean upon in getting us through the hard times. Jesus Christ is that Savior from God!

The Bible teaches us that God is one; there is only one God. It also teaches us that this one God shows Himself in three persons, the Father, the Son (Jesus), and the Holy Spirit, (see Deuteronomy 6:4 and Matthew 28:19). This works to our benefit. One of the main things we all need in life is a dependable Father, someone who can control situations and provide for our needs. God is that Father we all need. He loves us and blesses our lives. When we do wrong He disciplines us. We also need to identify with God, to connect with Him, to know that He understands us and is not just distant. Jesus came from God. He entered this world as a baby through the Virgin Mary rather than being born of man (see Matthew 1:23). Jesus had no sin nature from man to separate Him from God. He lived in this world of hardships just as we have to do. The Bible says He faced all the temptations we face but that He passed through this world without sinning (see Hebrews 4:14-15). He worked God the Father's will, standing up to injustice, healing the people, giving His sinless life in sacrifice to pay for the sins of the world. He was imprisoned, cruelly used, suffered and died on the cross for you and me. His innocent blood is now payment for the penalty of our sins (see 1Peter 2:24). God the Father raised Jesus from the dead and He lives as our Savior (see Acts 2:23-24 and 26). God has set Jesus as His 'Way' for mankind to return to Him and be saved. In John 14:6 Jesus said, "I am the way, the truth, and the life. No one comes to the Father except through Me." Where does Jesus live? How can I walk with Him? The third person of God the Holy Spirit has been sent by Jesus to live in the spirit of all those who receive Jesus as their Savior. The Holy Spirit is meant to be our Guide, our Comforter in this life being with us daily and connecting us with Father God and Jesus. The Holy Spirit reveals the things of Jesus to us and shows us how to live for God the way Jesus did when He lived as a man on earth (see John 16:13-15). You can begin your life again, God's way, by seeking God's forgiveness for your sins based on Jesus having died on the cross to pay the penalty for sin. You can ask God to save you through His Son Jesus Christ and He will save you from the ultimate penalty of sin and give you His Holy Spirit to guide you in His way of life.

If you have not already found these things out then you may need to search the Bible to gain confidence in what I am writing to you. I want to encourage you to do so because you really must know for yourself that Jesus is God's Way. It is not enough for you to hear it from me or someone else. If you have a Bible you must read and think about it for yourself. If you don't have a Bible then get one. If you can't get one then think over what is being said. God is real and He will reveal Himself and the reality of His plan of salvation to you if you will ask Him to do so. Go to God, tell Him that you want to know the truth and then start spending time reading and thinking about His word and talking to Him in prayer. As stated earlier, Jesus said, "And you shall know the truth, and the truth shall make you free", John 8:32.

Now do you really need salvation? What if you just settle for the life you have chosen, hard as it may be, difficult as it may be? Friend I want to tell you that God has had a lot of patience with mankind and not just mankind as a whole but you and me as individuals. God created this world and blessed us with it. He has looked for and expected better things in us than we have produced. In all man's long history we see that hatred, violence, pride, selfishness, and every evil thing captures our attention much easier than the things of God. We fall so easily into temptation and into justifying our behavior no matter how far from God's will it is. Yes, God looks for better things from us. His intention was for us to be members of His family, a people of His very own (see Titus 2:11-14). God is still looking for and holding out His salvation through Jesus to all those who will receive it and follow His Son Jesus, John 4:23-24 says, "But the hour is coming, and now is, when the true worshipers will worship the Father in spirit and truth; for the Father is seeking such to worship Him. God is Spirit, and those who worship Him must worship in spirit and truth". Those who turn their back on God or who simply continue in their own evil ways cannot expect God to welcome them into His family once they die. If we reject the 'Way' (Jesus) that God holds out to us sinners then we can have no hope or expectation of the eternal life He wants to share with us. Rather as the Bible says in Psalm 9:17 "The wicked shall be turned into hell, And all the nations that forget God". There is punishment coming for sin and on the sinner. The devil and his angels will be judged so don't think that you will escape if you continue to live a selfish, self directed life or if you try to build up your own righteousness apart from submission to God. Not only is Jesus God's Way. But He is the only way that leads to a right standing and right relationship with God. The whole man, whether he believes it or not, is sick with sin and evil (see Isaiah 1:4-5 and Romans 3:23). We all need to be saved from the destruction that is coming because of sin. I urge you to read the following Gospel message and take it to heart.

Chapter Two

The Gospel

Repentance and Remission of Sins

In Luke 24:47 we read the following words of Jesus: "That repentance and remission of sins should be preached in (My) name among all nations". What does Jesus mean by saying this?

Jesus, who had three days before this been condemned as a criminal, by jealous men, for not denying that He was the Christ, the Son of God (Matthew 26:63-65), had been mocked, beaten, spit on and cruelly crucified, had died on the cross, been buried and had now risen from the dead by the power of God Almighty spoke to His disciples (followers) and told them that they are to take the same message of peace with God that He had been preaching and share it with all nations.

Repentance-

Jesus had come preaching; "Repent, for the Kingdom of Heaven is at hand" (Matthew 4:17).

-"All we like sheep have gone astray; We have turned, every one, to his own way" (Isaiah 53:6a).

-"For all have sinned and fall short of the glory of God" (Romans 3:23).

-"For the wages of sin is death" (Romans 6:23).

-"The wicked shall be turned into hell, and all the nations that forget God" (Psalm 9:17).

-"...it is appointed for men to die once, but after this the judgment" (Hebrews 9:27).

"Follow Me" was Jesus' call to men to become His disciples (Matthew 4:19). "Come to Me, all you who labor and are heavy laden, and I will give you rest. Take My yoke upon you and learn from Me, for I am gentle and lowly in heart, and you will find rest for your souls. For My yoke is easy and My burden is light." (Matthew 11: 28-30).

"Let the wicked forsake his way, And the unrighteous man his thoughts; Let him return to the LORD, And He will have mercy on him; And to our God, For He will abundantly pardon." (Isaiah 55:7).

This is what Jesus means by repentance: to turn from your way and follow Him the Lord, becoming His disciple (follower), taking on His yoke (His leadership), learning of Him.

Remission of sins-

God the Son, born of God's Spirit and the virgin Mary, has come down in love to call us to Himself that we should follow Him out of our way, which leads to death and hell, into His way which leads to life with Him forevermore (John 3:16-17). And He Himself has made our repentance possible by bearing our sin on the cross to pay the penalty for it, (death and hell), that through faith in Him shown through repentance we might have pardon, the remission (be forgiven) of our sins (1 Peter 2:24; 2 Corinthians 5:20-21). "'Come now, and let us reason together,' Says the LORD, 'Though your sins are like scarlet, They shall be as white as snow'" (Isaiah 1:18 see 19-20).

To all Jesus says: "I am the way, the truth, and the life. No one comes to the Father except through Me. ... unless you repent you will all likewise perish. ...he who hears My word and believes in Him who sent Me has everlasting life, and shall not come into judgment, but has passed from death into life." (John 14:6, Luke 13:5, John 5:24 respectively).

-*Search* the Scriptures to see if the message you have just read is true.

-*Call* on God, (prayer), to lead you in knowing the truth about Jesus.

-*Follow* the Lord Jesus, repenting of your sins, receiving His sacrifice for your sins, giving yourself to be His disciple.

You shall find rest for your soul and life eternal.

John 3:16-19

"For God so loved the world that He gave His only begotten Son, that whoever believes in Him should not perish but have everlasting life. For God did not send His Son into the world to condemn the world, but that the world through Him might be saved. He who believes in Him is not condemned; but he who does not believe is condemned already, because he has not believed in the name of the only begotten Son of God. And this is the condemnation, that the light has come into the world, and men loved darkness rather than light, because their deeds were evil."

Chapter Three

This is what happened to me.
(a short testimony of my Salvation.)

I grew up in a seemingly normal home which lacked two things that I was not aware of. First, our family did not understand how to give and receive love. Second, our family was not focused on God. Around the time when I was ten years old my father left us and my mother began to look for truth through psychiatry. I chose an angry reaction to this and I made specific choices to harden myself to other people. I also began to experience strong feelings of being unwanted. Satan used these conflicts in my soul to begin to destroy me as a person. Throughout my teenage years I took my identity from hanging out with the guys on the streets and drowned myself in daily drug and alcohol use along with other foul habits. Those were harsh times. I had a bully who tormented me for years. I remember a few who were brave enough to try and tell us about Jesus. These 'Jesus Freaks' we abused, verbally and even physically. I had no idea what they would have said if I had listened because I never let them finish.

Life began to change for me when I tried to run away from it all by joining the Army in 1978 and going overseas. I remember feeling 'lost' because of separation from my gang and the new situation I was in. But really it was the beginning of Jesus starting to draw me to Himself. I remember thinking many times: 'why am I here on this earth and what is life really all about?' I took those questions through all my military training and overseas. One night, as I was laying on my bunk feeling very lost and thinking about these things, I saw a stack of Bibles next to the TV set. I remember saying to myself, 'I have cursed everyone who has tried to tell me about that book, I'm going to read it and see what it says.' I was pretty amazed at the things I began to find in the Bible, the same things I have shared with you. I took the Bible with me and began to read it.

One night while reading the Bible Jesus visited me in the Spirit, (I did not actually see Him but I knew He was there). He revealed to me who I was, who He was, and my need for His Salvation. I got up, locked my door, and got down on my knees and asked Him to save me. I remember thinking, 'what is going to happen now'? Nothing dramatic happened right then, but from that day on I have known in my heart that I am saved from my sins. I gained peace with God and eternal life through Jesus Christ my Lord. The other thing that changed is that my heart softened. I no longer felt that I had to put on the 'tough guy' act in order to face the world.

Part Two

Freedom from Slavery to Sin,

Jesus is the Truth!

Chapter Four

The Nature of Sin.

This chapter will begin to take you into the heart of how you can become free from slavery to repeating sin in your life through Jesus Christ. Before we get into the details of 'how' to break free I need to help you understand more about: the nature of sin in us, God's power in our lives, God's plan for our lives, and how to choose to start working with God to overcome sin. Please have patience and read it all. I know that many of you will just want to get to the part about how to do it.

Freedom from slavery to sin begins with understanding what has happened to us when we received God's Savior Jesus Christ and understanding the grace and power of God available to those who will follow Him. If you have not repented of your sins and received Jesus as your Lord and Savior then these words will not do you much good. Without Christ you are still on the outside looking in. But with Christ you have all the resources of every child of God. You will find God ready to work with you and He will answer your prayers. Of course that working is going to be in His time and those prayers will be answered according to His will and not yours. Remember, He is the Lord and you are the servant or child, not the other way around. The sooner you accept that it can and will only be done in His way and in His time the easier it will be for you.

As I mentioned before, the Bible teaches that God shows Himself to us in three persons, the Father, the Son, and the Holy Spirit. God is what we commonly call a trinity and in the very first chapter of the Bible God talks to Himself. In Genesis 1:26 He says, "Let Us make man in Our image, according to Our likeness..". We are made in His image and likeness and so it should not surprise us to find that we also are a trinity. We have three parts to ourselves, we have a body, we have a soul, and we have a spirit. Along with many Bible verses that talk about each of these parts, Paul the Apostle confirms this idea in his prayer for believers in 1 Thessalonians 5:23, "Now may the God of peace Himself sanctify you completely; and may your whole spirit, soul, and body be preserved blameless at the coming of our Lord Jesus Christ." Some teach, and I basically accept it, that our soul also has three parts, our mind, our will, and our emotions. I am going to explain why all of this is helpful to understand.

We have already seen that the Bible declares all of mankind to be sinners, "For all have sinned and fall short of the glory of God", (Romans 3:23). As we have also seen, this sinful condition separates us from God, "your sins have hidden His face from you," Isaiah 59:2. This applies to everyone no matter how 'clean' his or her life may look or be. Even the nicest guy who seems to love everyone and helps his neighbor is still a sinner, lost from God, unless he repents and receives the free gift of God's salvation through Jesus Christ. Remember our focus verse? John 14:6 "Jesus said to him, 'I am the way, the truth, and the life. No one comes to the Father except through Me.'" The gospel is clear, there is a way to God but it is also clear that no one gets there any other way, not by good works or good deeds or by making a deal with God. Why is this? The person who grew up in a good home, with good 'family' values, in a nation where the laws, for the most part, were based on God's word or other moral teachings has a good chance of becoming what we call a good person. The problem this person still has is not found in their body because the body alone does not sin all by itself. Neither is it mainly found in their soul (the mind, will, or emotions) which are largely shaped by how they chose to respond to their life, (good life, good family, good laws are more likely to help someone develop a 'good' soul). The main problem, which makes them a sinner, is found in their spirit. We might commit a sin with our body or with part of our soul but we are 'sinners' and lost from God because of the condition of our spirit.

In the 8th chapter of the book of Romans (Romans 8:9-11) we read: "Now if anyone does not have the Spirit of Christ, he is not His. And if Christ is in you, the body is dead because of sin, but the Spirit is life because of righteousness." There it is! When we receive Jesus as Lord and Savior the salvation we receive is the Spirit of Christ in our spirit. Our spirit is now alive because of Jesus Christ and His righteousness. In Ephesians 2:1 and 2:4-9 we read: "And you He made alive, who were dead in trespasses and sins... But God, who is rich in mercy, because of His great love with which He loved us, even when we were dead in trespasses, made us alive together with Christ (by grace you have been saved), and raised us up together, and made us sit together in the heavenly places in Christ Jesus, that in the ages to come He might show the exceeding riches of His grace in His kindness toward us in Christ Jesus. For by grace you have been saved through faith, and that not of yourselves; it is the gift of God, not of works, lest anyone should boast." So every person, no matter how good or bad, can only be saved by the grace of God. Grace means: undeserved favor, something we did not earn or deserve. We all start at the same place in Jesus, with our spirit being 'made alive' by the Spirit of Christ when we repent of our sinfulness and receive Him. As the book of John verse 1:12 says, "But as many as received Him, to them He gave the right to become children of God, to those who believe in His name: who were born, not of blood, nor of the will of the flesh, nor of the will of man, but of God." In these truths we find our help, our power to begin living for Jesus. He has made us alive, His Spirit is now in us; we have been declared righteous or not guilty because Jesus Christ the righteous one has paid the penalty for our sin. His innocent blood has been shed in place of ours. He took the death we rightly deserve and now God the Father has raised Him from the dead to be Lord and Savior sharing His righteousness with those who believe and receive Him. He does this by putting His Holy Spirit into our spirit raising us from spiritual death in Him. We have been given the right to become children of God. This is what has happened to us and now we are in a position to start doing and living the way God intended for us. Being alive in Christ we are no longer separated from God by a sinful nature in our spirit, He will hear us and will now help us. God's power is in our corner or rather we are in His corner now. Before this God was looking for us. But now we are found.

Now what about all the sins we still fall into so easily? What about the temptations I give into and the struggles that war within my soul? My mind is tormented with the evil that I remember. My emotions are difficult, I have depression, I have anger. Many times I cannot find the willpower to choose to do good. I'm just not like the lucky guy who grew up with a clean life.

First of all, if it is any comfort, I have known many people who have come to Jesus from what seems to be a pretty clean background. I thank God for them because, if willing, they are often able to help many people right away without having to clean up a really messy life first. Often though, they just have another set of difficulties, than you or I do, which they will have to grow up through. Sometimes, because they seem to be good persons, they don't see how truly awesome it is that God has had mercy on them. It can also be easier for them to fall into the sin of looking down on other people or judging other sinners more than themselves. 1 Timothy 5:24, "some men's sins are clearly evident, preceding them to judgment, but those of some men follow later."

The Bible makes it clear that all believers in Christ need to put to death the self-centered selfish part of us that was firmly in control before we were saved. (In reading the New Testament you will often hear of our self-centeredness being called the 'flesh' or our 'old man'.) In Mark 8:34-38 Jesus put it like this, "When He had called the people to Himself, with His disciples also, He said to them, 'Whoever desires to come after Me, let him deny himself, and take up his cross, and follow Me. For whoever desires to save his life will lose it, but whoever loses his life for My sake and the gospel's will save it. For what will it profit a man if he gains the whole world, and loses his own soul? Or what will a man give in exchange for his soul? For whoever is ashamed of Me and My words in this adulterous and sinful generation, of him the Son of Man also will be ashamed when He comes in the glory of His Father with the holy angels.'" The call of Christ is unmistakably a call to deny our 'self', take up our 'cross' (be crucified), and follow Him. The Apostle Paul put it like this in Galatians 2:20, "I have been crucified with Christ; it is no longer I who live, but Christ lives in me; and the life which I now live in the flesh I live by faith in the Son of God, who loved me and gave Himself for me."

In talking to many prisoners I have found that they take comfort in the words of Romans 7:15-18 "For what I am doing, I do not understand. For what I will to do, that I do not practice; but what I hate, that I do. If, then, I do what I will not to do, I agree with the law that it is good. But now, it is no longer I who do it, but sin that dwells in me."

I fully understand that we feel we need to find a reason for why we are still sinning even after receiving Jesus Christ. It is confusing for us as Christians when we still sin. So much preaching tells us to stop doing wrong. These verses would seem to say that it is not my fault, instead it is sin which lives in me, it is the fault of sin that I still do and think bad things. But we cannot simply stop at the end of these verses. In the next verses Romans 7:24-25 reads: "O wretched man that I am! Who will deliver me from this body of death? I thank God--through Jesus Christ our Lord! So then, with the mind I myself serve the law of God, but with the flesh the law of sin." Who will deliver us from this problem of continuing to sin, this body of death? God will deliver us through Jesus! Continuing in the very next chapter, Romans chapter 8, we read about how this will be done. Romans 8:10-11 says: "And if Christ is in you, the body is dead because of sin, but the Spirit is life because of righteousness. But if the Spirit of Him who raised Jesus from the dead dwells in you, He who raised Christ from the dead will also give life to your mortal bodies through His Spirit who dwells in you." Continuing in Romans 8:13-14, "For if you live according to the flesh you will die; but if by the Spirit you put to death the deeds of the body, you will live. For as many as are led by the Spirit of God, these are sons of God." So God has a plan for cleaning up our other parts. He starts with the spirit and says that by His Spirit we can put to death the deeds or sins of the body. The Spirit of God will lead us and show us how. God does not want us to make excuses about our continuing sin problems or to be discouraged because it is hard to kill our sins. God has a way. Further along in Romans chapter 8 verses 28-29 we read: "And we know that all things work together for good to those who love God, to those who are the called according to His purpose. For whom He foreknew, He also predestined to be conformed to the image of His Son, that He might be the firstborn among many brethren." That means that God intends to conform or make us like Jesus. We are not meant to remain in sin or to stay overcome by sin. We are now His sons and daughters and wherever we have to start from we are to grow up into the likeness of our big brother Jesus Christ.

We need to understand that when God says He will give life to our mortal bodies through His Spirit who dwells in us that he is talking about our body and our soul. Our body by itself does not sin apart from the choices we make or the things we allow it to do. With our body we may strike someone in anger but it is not our body alone that hates or gets angry. We hate or get angry in our soul where our mind and emotions are filled with the anger and then with our will we choose to attack or at least choose not to stop ourselves. The Bible is very clear about these things and speaks directly to them. In Ephesians 4:31-32 we see both our evil side and what God wants for our soul, "Let all bitterness, wrath, anger, clamor, and evil speaking be put away from you, with all malice. And be kind to one another, tenderhearted, forgiving one another, just as God in Christ forgave you." Bitterness, wrath, and anger are found down in our soul. They are in our mind and emotions. Clamor, which means arguing and fighting with words, and evil speaking are things we do with both our soul and body. The soul supplies the bitterness, wrath, and anger and the body is used to share it with someone else. The same thing is found in Colossians 3:8-10, "But now you yourselves are to put off all these: anger, wrath, malice, blasphemy, filthy language out of your mouth. Do not lie to one another, since you have put off the old man with his deeds, and have put on the new man who is renewed in knowledge according to the image of Him who created him".

My hope is that you now understand where our problem of continuing sin is found. Like our Creator, we are a trinity. We have a spirit, a soul, and a body. Through Jesus our spirit, which was dead towards God, is now alive but we still have these problems in our soul, which are expressed by our body. Understanding this we can now chose to begin dealing with it in God's truth by God's Spirit within us and find His freedom. The next two chapters will get into the 'how' of discovering and dealing with our continuing sin problem. Before this there are three things I think we need to address.

First, many of us need to understand about assurance of salvation. How do I stay saved or how can I really be saved if I still have sinful thoughts and continue to commit sinful acts? Salvation is like adoption, Galatians 4:4-6 says: "But when the fullness of the time had come, God sent forth His Son, born of a woman, born under the law, to redeem those who were under the law, that we might receive the adoption as sons. And because you are sons, God has sent forth the Spirit of His Son into your hearts, crying out, 'Abba, Father!'" (For the benefit of my women readers I want to make sure you understand that in Christ we are all equals and the Bible often uses the term sons of God to mean all believers, Galatians 3:28-29 states: "There is neither Jew nor Greek, there is neither slave nor free, there is neither male nor female; for you are all one in Christ Jesus.") Now when you adopt someone you take him or her in just as they are. We might know something about the child from the adoption agency but we won't know everything until we actually bring the child home to start living with us. We may have been told that they are very troubled or that they have done bad things and might do them again. We would understand that there will be work to do with that child if they are to understand love and learn to become loving to others. Now God already knows everything about us before he adopts us into His family. He knows about all of our sins and all of our pain and hurt. God knows what it will take to help each of us grow up into Christ and He knows how long it is going to take. He knows all of this ahead of time and He chooses to adopt us anyway. The Bible teaches that "He has made us accepted in the Beloved", Ephesians 1:6. Jesus was sent to save us while we were still sinners, not after we have been made perfect, Romans 5:8-9: "But God demonstrates His own love toward us, in that while we were still sinners, Christ died for us." Jesus taught us that it is not easy to get lost again once we are saved. In John 10:26-30 we read, "My sheep hear My voice, and I know them, and they follow Me. And I give them eternal life, and they shall never perish; neither shall anyone snatch them out of My hand. My Father, who has given them to Me, is greater than all; and no one is able to snatch them out of My Father's hand. I and My Father are one." Assurance or security of salvation is one of the birthrights for every Christian. We can rest assured that once we have received Jesus we are members of God's family and as Jesus said in John 6:37 "All that the Father gives Me will come to Me, and the one who comes to Me I will by no means cast out."

Now the Bible does talk about those who receive God and who then fall away. It says that they cannot be restored again. So potentially, even though no one can snatch me from God's hand, I could choose to reject Jesus and stop following Him or I could refuse to give up behaviors that God tells me I need to give up or I could even speak blasphemy against the Holy Spirit. I will give you the Bible verses here for those things if you are worried about them. (Hebrews 6:4-8, Galatians 5:16-26, Matthew 12:31-32, 2 Peter chapter 2.) Jesus talks about those who fall away as seed that sprang up quickly but had no root, when hard times came because of knowing Jesus they turned away, (Matthew 13:20-21). Personally, I doubt that anyone who has fallen away from God to the point where they cannot be restored would have read this far. The words I am being led to write are for those who are still interested and still seeking God. What you really need to know is that if you are still letting God work in you and still wanting to learn and follow the Lord Jesus then it does not matter how many times you have failed or stumbled into sin. God did not save you and adopt you into His family because you were perfect or because you would be the best child or because you never fail or stumble. He saved you because He loves you. God knows you are a sinner, a failure on your own, one who stumbles into sin and needs to be saved. He loves you. My advice is to stop worrying about whether you are still saved and chose to go forward in Christ, follow Him! That is how you will get to where God wants to take you.

Second, many of us get discouraged and end up giving up. What we need to understand about ourselves is that we are a work in progress. It took a long time for us to get this way and it may take a long time for us to get free from it. My personal experience has been that God has His own idea of what we are to work on when and how long it will take. In His mercy He has not demanded that I work on everything all at once but has shown me one thing at a time. God has been dealing with me and making me more free over the last twenty-six or more years. He worked on the big stuff that was keeping me from any other progress first, like drug addiction. Then we moved on to the deeper things of my soul like hatred, fears, and other controlling issues. From there He had other work to do. God sees us as a work in progress like raising a son or daughter. The child learns to eat, then to crawl, then to walk, and so on until we are mature adults in Christ able to both give and receive His love. Often we think of ourselves as all bad. If we are doing good and then one bad thing or one stumble happens we trash the whole thing, what's the use of trying, and head back into sin. What we need to do is accept ourselves where we are at, because God does, and then when we fail or stumble into sin be honest with ourselves and with God, confess the sin, receive His forgiveness, and move forward in Christ again. When Joshua was told to take over the promised land for the children of Israel God told him something interesting, in Deuteronomy 7:21-24 we read: "And the LORD your God will drive out those nations before you little by little; you will be unable to destroy them at once, lest the beasts of the field become too numerous for you. But the LORD your God will deliver them over to you, and will inflict defeat upon them until they are destroyed. And He will deliver their kings into your hand, and you will destroy their name from under heaven; no one shall be able to stand against you until you have destroyed them." In the same way God will drive out the sin that has a hold on your soul and body, little by little, not all at once, none of them will be able to stand before you, they will all be destroyed. The king of hate and the king of lust, the king of perversion and the king of addiction, all of them are going down as you remain encouraged or return to encouragement in Christ and let God work His patient work of grace, truth, and time within you.

Third, breaking free from slavery to sin is not always easy. It will challenge you and stretch you beyond what you have chosen for yourself. To work with God in cleaning up our mess of sin we will have to let a lot of things die which we have had around for a long time, as Jesus died, so that God can raise you from the dead in those areas of your life as He raised Christ from the dead. You have to want it. When you as a Christian, saved by the grace of God, really decide that you want to be free from slavery to sin in order to be free to serve the living God then nothing can stop God from healing you. The real question is: do you want to be free? In John 5:5-7 Jesus asks a curious question, "Now a certain man was there who had an infirmity thirty-eight years. When Jesus saw him lying there, and knew that he already had been in that condition a long time, He said to him, 'Do you want to be made well?'" The man was sick for 38 years and Jesus asked him if he wanted to be made well. Not everyone does, some have made a friend of their sickness, they are comfortable or think they are more comfortable in their sin or sickness than if they got free. We cannot hang onto our sick, sinful life and also grow up in the life of Jesus that God wants us to have, we have to make a choice. Do you want to be free?

"And you shall know the truth, and the truth shall make you free", John 8:32
Jesus said to him, 'I am ... the truth ...', from John 14:6

Chapter Five

Finding the Roots of Our Sin.

Why is it that we often end up doing what we should not do? For most of us this happens on a regular basis. We either know we should not do it but choose to anyway or we do wrong things so quickly and automatically that there is not even time for choice to enter into the question.

If I have an apple tree and it is full of fruit what kind of fruit is it? An apple tree always brings forth apples. If I pick off all the apples so that there is no fruit then what kind of a tree do I have? Even without the apples it is still an apple tree and will grow more apples next season. The reason the apple tree continues to bear apples is because of the roots and the tree not because of the apples. Sin is very much like a fruit. You can pick all the fruit on the tree but it will grow again. It does not grow again because of the fruit but because of the tree and it's roots. We have come to Christ for salvation but we still have problems in our souls that bear bad fruit. We have much misunderstanding in our minds, we still have hurt and painful memories and emotions, we still strive to do things our own way in our will. Our reaction to these ends up being our choices to sin. Some of this sin fruit is so bad that, even though we are Christians, it gets us into trouble and can land us in prison. The Holy Spirit will begin to challenge these things in the Christian, who is now saved by the grace of God, so that He can bring us into the maturity of Christ.

My main point is that sin is a fruit. You can pick the fruit but it will probably grow again. You can quit drinking or using drugs but the forces that drive you to do so will still be there. You need to work together with the Holy Spirit to get at the root of each problem. Once you find the root of the problem and pull out that root then the fruit of sin will stop and you will be free from that particular problem.

There are actually four words in the Bible that we commonly think of as sin. The words are: sin, trespass, transgression, and iniquity. Some of the newer Bible translations have used the word sin to cover most of these. However, the differences between these words are important to understand.

Sin means to 'miss the mark' or 'to fall short'. We often hear people talk about not measuring up, 'I don't measure up' or 'you don't measure up'. Usually that has to do with meeting someone else's expectation. In comparison to a Holy God none of us measure up, we all sin and 'fall short' of the Glory of God, Romans 3:23 "for all have sinned and fall short of the glory of God". Sin can be a simple thing with minor consequences or something really bad but either way it is simply a failure, a falling short of what should have been. For example, if I am holding a cup of hot coffee and someone bumps me and it spills on a person in front of me something has just happened that should not have happened. It is no big deal to simply apologize for it but I cannot undo it and there are consequences like stained clothes or a burn. On the other hand if I accidentally run over someone with my car they may die or become crippled and I might even go to jail, that sin has much bigger consequences but is still 'falling short' of what should have been. It was an unintentional accident caused by their failure or mine or a combination of both. It should not have happened.

Trespass is a little different that simple sin. With trespassing we know the rule or the law ahead of time but choose to break it anyway. Like entering a building when there is a no trespassing sign on it. The law may be from God's word the Bible or from our society which God's word tells us to obey, Romans 13:1-2 "Let every soul be subject to the governing authorities. For there is no authority except from God, and the authorities that exist are appointed by God." Either way trespass is a more serious action than the failure of sin because we are making a choice perhaps to steal or to kill, to break the Lord's rules in some way.

Transgression means to revolt or rebel. When we are living in rebellion against God because He has asked us to do something and we will not or He wants us to make some changes in our lives but we will not, then we are transgressing. Notice that this both this and trespass have to do with the part of our soul we call our will. This is also very serious because we are making a choice to say no to God. He will probably put our prayers and spiritual growth on hold until we are willing to follow Him again. That is what any good father would do.

Iniquity is the most important word we are going to look at when it comes to breaking the cycle of sin in our lives. It is not a word we use commonly and is mainly found in the Old Testament of the Bible. In the New Testament the same idea is brought out in the word 'wickedness'. Iniquity or wickedness means 'a moral evil or perversity'. Iniquities are the evil and perverse qualities within us that end up being expressed as sins, trespasses, or transgressions. Notice now that sin, trespass, and transgression are fruits. If they are very simple, like the spilled coffee, then they might be picked off through apologizing and will probably not come back. But if they are very complicated, having to do with how we feel about ourselves or with how we think or with our will, then if we pick these fruits off they will grow again. Maybe next time the sin or trespass will be worse but it is the same root of iniquity or wickedness that will make it grow. Many people are separated from the opportunity to commit certain sins or trespasses by time in prison. They may even follow the Lord while in prison, but return to the sin or trespass once they get out because they never dealt with the root cause of their sin. So many times in church services or by well meaning Christians we are told to stop sinning. In many cases unless we deal directly with the iniquity or wickedness that is driving the sins then we will not be able to stop. In my own life there have been many examples of this. God helped me to pick the fruit of drug abuse but I was not able to stop my drive towards self-destructive behaviors until He helped me to deal with the root of the problem, which was a deep feeling and belief of worthlessness and self-hatred.

The bad news is that much iniquity is inherited. In giving Moses the Ten Commandments the Lord adds in Exodus 20:5, "For I, the LORD your God, am a jealous God, visiting the iniquity of the fathers on the children to the third and fourth generations of those who hate Me". (See also Numbers 14:18 and Deuteronomy 5:9.) I need to pause here for a moment to mention that many newer Bible translations will read 'punishing the children for the sins of the fathers'. However, the original Hebrew word for visiting is paqad, which means to visit with friendly or hostile intent, it does not mean to punish. Also the original Hebrew word for iniquity is 'avon, which means perversity or moral evil and does not have the same concept as 'sin' which means to fall short. I fear that the important concept of iniquity has been hidden in many of the other passages of these translations as well. So God 'visits' the iniquity of the fathers on the children to the third and fourth generation of those who hate Him. Sometimes we see this in very direct ways such as alcoholism or anger or abusive behavior, which seems to stay in a family from one generation to the next. Other times the iniquity is a little harder to understand, especially if it was visited through the actions of a grandfather you never knew who hated God. From what I have learned about God over the years, I know that God wants His sons and daughters to grow out of these things and into the image of Christ. From that knowledge I believe He visits these iniquities because He is looking for someone in the family line who will break the cycle of them. I can't prove this last point but that is what I believe is going on. We can surely trust God that there is a good reason for this visitation and we do know that He does not want these things to continue in our family line.

The good news is that Jesus Christ is the truth that sets us free from not only sins but iniquity and wickedness as well. In the Old Testament book of Isaiah we have a very complete prophecy about the coming of Jesus and what He would do, written 700 years before He was born. In this prophecy are the following verses: Isaiah 53:5-6 "He was wounded for our transgressions, He was bruised for our iniquities; the chastisement for our peace was upon Him, and by His stripes we are healed. All we like sheep have gone astray; we have turned, every one, to his own way; And the LORD has laid on Him the iniquity of us all.",

Isaiah 53:11 "By His knowledge My righteous Servant shall justify many, For He shall bear their iniquities.", Isaiah 53:12 "And He bore the sin of many, And made intercession for the transgressors." If you read the whole of chapter 53 you will see that this one who is foretold as bearing our sin, transgressions, and iniquity dies and then gets to live again! Isaiah 53:9, "they made His grave with the wicked--But with the rich at His death", Isaiah 53:10-11, "He shall see His seed, He shall prolong His days, and the pleasure of the LORD shall prosper in His hand. He shall see the labor of His soul, and be satisfied." This then is more of the fullness that Jesus Christ has done for us through His death on the cross and resurrection from the dead. We are to understand that He has not only become the way of salvation for sin and from sins but also the way for forgiveness and cleansing from iniquity or wickedness, the moral evil and perversity in us that so often drives us to commit sins. As we identify the truth about those things in ourselves we can bring them to Jesus and gain freedom and complete cleansing from the bondage they bring. I want to encourage you that whenever you find sin in your life that is difficult to quit or seems like you just try and fail over and over again, start asking God to reveal the reason for why you are driven or attracted to that sin or trespass. We know from the word that our bodies are the temple of the Holy Spirit and that we are not to destroy the temple, 1 Corinthians 3:16. Why then are so many of us enslaved to things which destroy or defile our bodies, alcohol, drugs, smoking, prostitution, homosexuality and more? To become free from many of these things that we are enslaved to we will have to find the root which is bearing the fruit, the iniquity that brings this out in us.

Not all iniquity or wickedness can be traced back to our forefathers; we also bring it on ourselves through our own bad choices. However a large part is 'visited' on us by God because it was in our forefathers and we need to understand how to deal with that part. The people of God in the Old Testament times were taught and understood this concept as we see in the following verses. In speaking to the Israelites about a future time when they would rebel against God the Lord tells them about the disasters that are going to come on them for this rebellion. He continues to speak about how life will be for them, (it can be compared to many of our situations). Then He shows them the way back to life with Him. Let's read it from Leviticus 26:39-43, "And those of you who are left shall waste away in their iniquity in your enemies' lands; also in their fathers' iniquities, which are with them, they shall waste away. But if they confess their iniquity and the iniquity of their fathers, with their unfaithfulness in which they were unfaithful to Me, and that they also have walked contrary to Me, and that I also have walked contrary to them and have brought them into the land of their enemies; if their uncircumcised hearts are humbled, and they accept their guilt-- then I will remember My covenant with Jacob, and My covenant with Isaac and My covenant with Abraham I will remember; I will remember the land". Here we see that they are in trouble, bearing the fruit of rebellion or transgression against God and being punished for it. God refers to the root of their rebellion as their iniquity and the iniquity of their fathers. God also tells them how to get free from the iniquity: if they confess their iniquity and the iniquity of their fathers, with their unfaithfulness to Me, that they have walked contrary to Me, if their hearts are humbled, and they accept their guilt. Then I will remember! We can add to this the knowledge that Jesus Christ will bear our iniquity as we learned from Isaiah chapter 53. We have a Savior ready to take it and a Father God calling us to repentance from it.

Chapter Six

Breaking Free from Specific Iniquity.

Now let's make a connection through an example from my own life and then I will share with you the prayer I use to break the power of iniquities and wickedness I find causing the fruits of sin to grow in my life. One of the most difficult areas of wickedness that I have had rooted in me was 'the fear of man' which is a form of idolatry. I have found myself over the years doing things I should not do, allowing things I should not allow, not doing things I should do all because of what some other person 'might' then do in response. In short I lived in fear of others and I let that fear control my behavior. I did not say certain things to my wife or tell her how I really felt or let what I wanted be known because I was afraid she would get angry or withhold love from me or possibly leave me. I would not correct my children when they needed it or confront bad behavior in them because I was afraid of loosing a connection with them. When I was younger I allowed bullies to continue to harass me rather than standing up to them because I was afraid of what they would do.

I know that many of us share this same experience of the fear of man. It is not something that you can see by looking at a person because we hide it very well; after all we are 'afraid' that others will think we are weak. The person themselves can go for years living in this fear of man without connecting it as the reason why they do or don't do certain things, maybe there is only the inner sense that we are not living life to the fullest. There were actually a few different reasons for this fear in me but they all added up to the iniquity or wickedness of me letting someone else be Lord rather that letting Jesus be Lord of my life. Focusing in on the main root regarding my family the Lord showed me that I was behaving this way because I was afraid of loosing them. Why was I afraid of loosing my family Lord? Because you lost your first family through divorce when you were a child. Your father left the family and your mother left into her own world of psychoanalysis. Here then was the reason for the fear. I could now 'see' that I had been expecting the same bad thing to happen again and had been using behaviors of fear to try and prevent it from happening. In short I was not facing my problems with my wife and kids based on present reality but based on past events and was then using bad behavior motivated by fear as a tool to get things to go the way I wanted. Needless to say things were not getting better between all of us. I had to take responsibility for my iniquity of idolatry, for living in the fear of man (my family) rather than trusting in God. I had to pull this root of idolatry in order to stop bearing the fruit of living by a motivation of fear, which had the fruit of doing what I should not, allowing what I should not, and not doing what I should. I don't know if my forefathers had exactly the same problem although I remember my grandfather doing a lot of things because my grandmother would get angry if he did not. Whether it was a generational iniquity or not the remedy is the same.

Steps for Breaking the Hold of Iniquity.

First, understand that God does want us to take responsibility for and renounce iniquities (wickedness) whether found in our generational heritage or started by us, (read: Jeremiah 16:10-12).

Next, Work with the Lord to identify the iniquity causing the problem in your life. For example you may harbor racial hatred without having been personally hurt by anyone of that race. This has most likely been visited on you because one of your ancestors did not deal with it. Don't search for iniquities just for their own sake. If you are having a problem with ungodly actions, speech, or thought in your life then consider that it is possibly from a past hurt or iniquity and work with the Lord to look for it. You may need the help and counsel of other Christians in these efforts.

Lastly, take the matter to the Lord in prayer and finish it off with Him. Be bold and pray with faith knowing that Jesus came to set you free. Following are some steps in prayer to guide you, of course God will hear your prayer from your heart and the exact words are not as important as the fact that you are coming to Him for freedom.

Steps in Prayer:
1. Father in heaven I take responsibility on behalf of my forefathers, and myself for... (State the iniquity, in my example it was idolatry and fear of man).
2. I confess that this (name it) is sinful moral evil within me and I repent of it. I ask you for forgiveness and for cleansing by the blood of Jesus.

Note: Give some time for the emotions of godly sorrow over this evil to take place. Ask the Holy Spirit to help you with this.

3. I renounce this iniquity. I speak the punishment for this iniquity off of myself and on to my Lord Jesus, (He shall bear their iniquities, Isaiah 53:11).

4. I break the curse and power of those things off of my life and the lives of my children and I set myself and my children free from the punishment of those things in Jesus name.

Chapter Seven

Cleansing from Past Hurts.

**(Breaking free from the common
iniquity of un-forgiveness.)**

All of us have some measure of past hurts in our lives.
Many of us seem to have more than our share. Rejection
or actual abandonment by a Mother or Father is one of
the main sources but there are many others. Physical,
sexual, or emotional abuse can leave very deep hurts that
will bear bad fruit in our lives. Hurts can run deep, what
happens is we end up believing lies about our own worth
and value. If we were degraded through abuse we tend
to turn around and degrade others or at least ourselves.
The great news is that we have a Father in heaven Who
has demonstrated that He loves all of us and will accept
us into His family through salvation found in Jesus.
In fact, as may even be true in our own case, God has
demonstrated that He is willing to love and accept people
who have committed the worst sorts of crimes against
others. Should it be any wonder then that this loving God
who has called us to salvation and now calls us to grow

up into the example and image of His Son Jesus wants us to face and deal with the past hurts in our lives caused by others? Should it be any wonder if He wants us to come to forgive them for what they have done? In fact this is God's path of cleansing us from the damage caused by these same hurts.

We have the story in Matthew 18:21-35 which starts with Peter's question, "Lord, how often shall my brother sin against me, and I forgive him?" Jesus tells of a servant who owed his master a huge debt and was to be sold to pay it back. This is a word picture of the debt we owe God because of sin. The servant cried to the master for mercy as we have cried out to God for salvation. The master gave the servant mercy and forgave the debt setting him free. God has had mercy on us freeing us from the punishment of sin through His Son Jesus Christ. This servant went out and found a fellow servant who owed him money and demanded it. He put his fingers around the other servant's throat and choked him saying, 'pay me what you owe'! We often continue to hold other people responsible for the 'debts' they owe us, the sin they did against us. The fellow servant could not pay so the servant had him thrown into prison. People often cannot repay us for the sin they did to us, they cannot reverse the spiritual or emotional damage of serious sins. What do we do? We keep them in the prison of un-forgiveness. When the master found out about this he was angry, (verse 32-33) "You wicked servant! I forgave you all that debt because you begged me. Should you not also have had compassion on your fellow servant, just as I had pity on you?" God looks at our un-forgiveness in the same way. God has had incredible mercy on us in Christ through the salvation of our very souls and He expects us to extend that same forgiveness to all others no matter what they have done to us. Jesus ends the story by saying that the servant was delivered to torture until he should repay his debt. We are often in torture of past hurts continuing to believe lies about ourselves, continuing in bad fruits of emotional and physical expression that come from a wounded soul. These things continue until we work with God to examine what was done in the past, face it for what it is and deal with it. Jesus ends the story saying, (verse 35) "So My heavenly Father also will do to you if each of you, from his heart, does not forgive his brother his trespasses." Yes God will do this even to His saved children because He wants us to work through these things, forgive, and get well again.

Now some will say to me that Paul taught us not to look at the past. In Philippians 3:13-14 Paul wrote: "one thing I do, forgetting those things which are behind and reaching forward to those things which are ahead, I press toward the goal for the prize of the upward call of God in Christ Jesus". Many have used this passage to say that they don't have to look at their past. I feel for them, in actuality it takes a brave person to take a serious look at their own past and to let God heal them of past hurts. If you really want to do as Paul did and press on in the 'upward call of God in Christ Jesus' then you are committing yourself to God's plan for yourself, which, as I have shown, is for you to become like His Son Jesus. So by all means press on, but know this, that as you go forward in Christ you will continually bump into your own sins, and hurts, especially the deep ones that are still affecting your behaviors. Whether fits of rage, anger, depression, abuse of others, abuse of self, or whatever else, these behaviors are standing in the way of you becoming Christ like. So if you don't come to grips with those parts of your past, spending the time with God to find the roots causing the fruit, then you will not grow in those areas of your life. I do not say that someone should do nothing but look at their past. All I'm saying is that when we press on in Christ we will bump right into the effects of our past. When this happens to you have the courage to deal with it. I met one man behind bars who was obviously homosexual. He was about 40 years old and had recently come to Jesus for salvation. He told me that he knew letting other men abuse him sexually was wrong but was not sure how to break free. When I asked him how he first started into homosexuality he told me about being sexually used and abused by men during his childhood. He was still very angry about the abuse and with those men. He still had his fingers around their throat saying, 'pay me what you owe'! I encouraged him, if he really wanted to be free from his drive to abuse himself with homosexuality his first step needs to be spending the time with God to forgive the sinners who had hurt him like that. I hope he did.

In the book of 1 John 2:1 we read, "My little children, these things I write to you, so that you may not sin. And if anyone sins, we have an Advocate with the Father, Jesus Christ the righteous." An advocate is someone who stands up for you, someone who speaks on your behalf, someone who takes the part of a lawyer. Now you may have had good lawyers in the past or you may have had bad ones but now you have Jesus Christ the righteous one as your Advocate. How can Jesus help you with past hurts? How can He advocate for your freedom from the emotional and spiritual damage people have caused you? How can Jesus be the truth that sets you free? To make a long story as short as possible, remember that in Exodus 3:13-14 Moses stood before the burning bush and asked God what His name was. In Exodus 3:14 we read, "And God said to Moses, 'I AM WHO I AM.' And He said, 'Thus you shall say to the children of Israel, 'I AM has sent me to you.''" The original Hebrew word for this name of God means: the existing one or the one who is. In Hebrew the word is Yahweh, which is commonly used through our English Old Testament as the word 'LORD'. A number of times through the Old Testament God or others talk of who He is using His name, this name I AM. David did so when he said in Psalm 23, 'The LORD is my Shepherd'. In other words 'I AM is my Shepherd'. Looking at it further, it is God's very nature to shepherd us, to look out for us as a people who need to be cared for. Other verses are: 'I AM the LORD who heals you', 'The LORD is there', 'The LORD our righteousness', 'The LORD who sanctifies us', and 'In the mount of the LORD it shall be seen (or provided)'. All of these and more show us that it is God's nature, part of who He is, to shepherd, heal, be there for us, be our righteousness, sanctify us (set us apart for Himself), and provide for us. Now what does this have to do with Jesus and healing from past hurts? We have already covered the Biblical concept of Jesus being one of the three persons of God. In Philippians chapter 2 we see that Jesus being God choose to take on the form of man so He could come down and give Himself for us. While He was here, Jesus used the same concept of 'I AM' when speaking about himself. Among other sayings in the New Testament Jesus said the following: 'I am the bread of life', 'I am the door, if any enter by me he shall be saved', 'I am the light of the world he that follows me will not walk in darkness', along with our focus verse from John 14:6, "Jesus said to him, 'I am the way, the truth, and the life. No one comes to the Father except through Me.'" Jesus defined Himself through these and many other 'I AM' sayings in the New Testament. It's not that God will give you bread, light, a door, truth, life, etc. It's that God in Christ Jesus 'IS' the bread, light, door, truth, way, and all those other things. The Jewish leaders of His day were angry that He would compare Himself to

God in this way. On one occasion they wanted to stone Him to death for it. Out of all of His 'I AM' sayings what did He say that made them that angry? In John 8:53-59 the Jews challenged Jesus asking if He thought He was greater than Abraham or the prophets who were all dead long ago. It was Jesus reply in verse 58 that made them really angry, "Jesus said to them, 'Most assuredly, I say to you, before Abraham was, I AM.'" Jesus declared that even before Abraham, who they counted as the father of their nation, had ever existed, that He Jesus still exists, the I AM, the existing one is! That's as short as I can make a long story in order to give you a biblical basis for the fact that our God is not in time like we are. We are in time and cannot go back but our God is not! Jesus is the great I AM, the existing one who is not bound by time. Before Abraham was He still is. Jesus can still see your past. Even though you cannot, He can still be there at the moment when you were hurt, at the moment you were abandoned or abused. Because of this He can bring to you the knowledge of what happened, how you reacted to it, and how those decisions are still affecting your life. Or Jesus can work backwards with you from bad behaviors, the fruit you now have, to where it came from and how. This gives us the power of an Advocate who can truly help us to work through and overcome past hurts.

I need to cover one more thing about this subject of past hurts before we get into an example from my life and a method for working with God to deal with these problems. A person who is mature in Christ, which you and I are becoming, has a better understanding of sin and sinners and why people do the things that they do. When people hurt some one who has a proper understanding of these things then that person will likely be sooner to forgive than to allow the hurt to affect their life for the long term. The best example of this is Jesus Himself who was crucified and said 'Father forgive them for they do not know what they do', (Luke 23:34). He did not count it against them nor did He let the abuse twist Him inside taking on anger, depression, bitterness or the like. Unfortunately much of the wrong that has been done to us has been done when we were not mature, either not mature in Christ or when we were children, unequipped to handle what was done to us. In this case we made decisions because of the abuse. Decisions that have bound us either in anger and un-forgiveness or in believing we are no good or unlovable. These decisions have bound us emotionally and spiritually and have gone on to bear bad fruit of abusing and dishonoring ourselves and or others. Coming to the point, it is impossible for us to live a life where no bad things ever happen to us. What is important then is not what happens to us but how we respond to what happens to us. If we respond in a Godly way, with Godly decisions, in the way of Christ, not repaying evil for evil, forgiving as we have been forgiven, then our soul walks free from the hurt and God can heal it quickly. If we respond in ways that are not Godly and not of Christ then we stay bound by the hurt and it will bear bad fruit in our lives.

I have already shared about finding that deep feelings and belief of worthlessness and self-hatred were the roots of self-destructive behaviors in my life. These feelings were expressed in heavy drug abuse to cover the pain, shame and fears. When through God's help I finally quit the drugs, I still had to work with the Spirit of God and with some other Christians who cared about me to discover the reasons behind the feelings and beliefs. We should ask God to reveal such things to us, He will then choose to speak in our spirit or bring people into our lives, fellow Christians, a counselor, maybe a program. Our job is to stay open to how God will answer. (I want to be clear at this point that, if you have been prescribed medication for depression or some other emotional illness, I am not saying that medication should always be avoided in dealing with problems or that you should stop your medication. I do believe that medication should not be all that gets done. Be willing to work with God to find the reason behind the problem and be patient because He may want to work on other things first.) I had started acting out in self-destructive behavior, mostly drug and alcohol abuse, when I was eleven years old. This would take it's course over the next ten years all the way through to heroin addiction. It was actually two and a half years after I first came to Christ that He was able to lead me gently out of the addiction. Partly because I did not know much about the life my new Savior had for me and partly because I was still using the drugs to cover up my emotional pain. Within the next few years after this the Lord had delivered me from many outwardly dirty habits and was ready to start on the inside of me. At this time His Spirit began to confront my improper emotions and feelings about myself. With the help of some friends in my church elders group I was able to come to grips with and overcome these issues.

Basically, when I was 9 or 10 my parents divorced. Our family was pulled apart by the divorce. Each one of us went our separate ways emotionally if not moving out. I can remember when my dad told me he would not be coming home again. I can remember making an emotional decision at that time not to open myself up to anyone anymore. Not to let anyone have the opportunity to hurt me. Over the next few years the distance grew between my parents and myself. This brought me to a conclusion that my father did not want me. In fact on an emotional level I believed that he hated me and wished I had not been born. I began to believe that I really was worthless and I began to hate myself and engage in self-destruction. I spent my time hanging out with people who were mean to me. I drowned myself nightly in alcohol. I used stronger and harder drugs on a daily basis year by year. I looked for love in all the wrong places. Now after I was saved, when the Spirit of God was able to peel away the layers of self-protection, (this took some time), we discovered that the things I had believed about myself were lies, they were simply not true.

First of all I am loved and have infinite value in the eyes of my Creator God. Second of all my father certainly did not hate me. I have since learned that my father is actually a pretty good guy. He made many mistakes in his life, even sinned against his family through abandonment. He is the one who will have to face and deal with those things between himself and God. My job was to freely forgive him as Christ had freely forgiven me, to take my judgment off of him and let him go free. What had happened for me was that I had made wrong decisions about truth based on my immaturity, my ungodliness, and my emotional feeling rather than based on God's truth. I became clean from these past hurts and healed to the point where I am certainly not self-destructive anymore. In fact I rather like myself, which frees me up to love other people. There would be a number of other hurts, which I would discover later, all in God's time, but this had been a big one and the result was life changing.

Following is a method I learned and which you can use to work through the past hurts in your life.

Cleansing from Past Hurts

Symptoms of: anger, depression, lack of the good fruit of God's Holy Spirit (love, joy, peace, etc.), inability to hold relationships, or ungodly behaviors which you cannot seem to stop even though you want to stop show that there is a root cause for these things which needs to be healed. Seek the Lord to show you the root cause. It may be related to past rejection, abuse, or some other hurt. (It may be iniquity, which we have already covered.) He will bring to you the connections through His Spirit by revelation, remembrance, dreams, counseling, or other ways. Be patient, as the answers need to be in God's time not yours. Often an objective look at the situation is helpful. Ask yourself why you behave this way or why you have these feelings and continue to ask why every time the question of why is answered. This can lead you to a root reason at the bottom of it all. Example: I never stood up for my wife but always let others get away with insulting her. This caused great problems in our relationship. Why didn't or why couldn't I stand up for her even when I wanted to? God showed me that I had let my friends repeatedly insult my mother when I was young. Why? I wanted to let my mother get hurt. Why? Because I felt she deserved to get hurt because I felt hurt and rejected by her. This last answer was the root cause of why I couldn't stand up for my wife because it is where I was still holding bitterness and un-forgiveness towards my mother.

Next identify any life decisions you made as a result of this hurt, rejection, or abuse having come into your life.

We respond to every situation with choices. We either make godly or ungodly choices. My decision to make sure my mother was hurt because I felt she had rejected me was an ungodly life decision, which shaped my behavior well beyond the time of hurt. Again let God make the connections as above, showing you the decisions you made as a result of the hurt, the abuse or rejection. Examples: Someone very important rejects you and you decide: 'I'll never let anyone hurt me again'. You are physically or sexually abused by a family member and you decide: 'I'm not good for anything but abuse'. These decisions can be made directly or emotionally but they go on to affect our lives.

Steps in Prayer:
1. Invite Jesus to go with you back to the time when the original hurt or hurts happened. ("Before Abraham was I AM", John 8:58. Jesus is there in the past.)
2. Remember with Jesus what happened and tell Jesus how you feel or felt about it.
   Note: Many of us have buried our emotions concerning these things. It is very important to bring together the remembrance of the hurt with the emotions that were experienced. Ask the Holy Spirit to help you with this.
3. Forgive all those involved in the rejection or abuse (Matthew 6:14-15), forgive others, forgive yourself, forgive God, (wait for the Holy Spirit to show you who was involved because it is not always clear). Name them specifically with what they did, I forgive you (mom) for (leaving me).
4. Take your judgment off of them and set them free from the un-forgiveness you have held. I take my judgment off of you (name them) and set you free. (Matthew 7:1)
5. Confess and forsake the ungodly life decision(s) you made as a result of the hurt, (Proverbs 28:13). Choose at this time to love that person or persons and declare the godly choice you should have made. (Again the Lord can show you what would have been a godly decision in the face of that hurt.) Note: Having a godly decision to replace

the ungodly one(s) which were made is very important, (see Mathew 12:43-45).

6. By prayer bind the enemy (the devil), (Ephesians 6:12), who has been able to get to you through this hurt and un-forgiveness to attack you.

Note: If you find later that a tormenting spirit will not leave you then ask God if there is some right which you have yielded by which that spirit gained legal entry to your life. (Adam gave up his earthly kingdom to Satan by his ungodly life decision to disobey God, Genesis chapter 3.) Deal with this as you would with other ungodly life decisions, (see #5 above).

7. Ask the Holy Spirit to please cleanse, heal, and seal this area where you had been wounded.

Chapter Eight,

The First Commandment with a Promise.

Now that we are better prepared to deal with iniquity and past hurts we need to look at a subject that is a common problem for most of us.

We all have a father and a mother who affected our lives greatly either for good, for evil, or for both. We may never have met them or they may have been with us every day. They may still be alive or they may now be dead. They may have shown us love and kindness or they may have made us feel worthless. Their hands, their words, may have been loving or abusive or maybe it was the lack of any touch or words at all. You can think about your own parents, your lack of parents, or even important foster parents, adoptive parents, or close family members who did the job of bringing you up. Almost without exception, when you find a person who is struggling with continuing sin in their life and who keeps bringing forth bad fruit, you will find someone whose relationship with their father or mother or parent is not or was not well.

The fifth commandment of the Ten Commandments found in Deuteronomy 5:16 reads like this: "Honor your father and your mother, as the LORD your God has commanded you, that your days may be long, and that it may be well with you in the land which the LORD your God is giving you." The apostle Paul points out that this is the first of the Ten Commandments that has a promise connected to it, Ephesians 6:2-3 "'Honor your father and mother,' which is the first commandment with promise: 'that it may be well with you and you may live long on the earth.'"

We can approach this from another way by asking the question: Is it well with you? How is your life going for you? What is your emotional health like? If the answer to those questions is negative rather than positive then ask yourself: How is my relationship with my father, mother, or parent? If they are dead or no longer connected to you then how was your relationship? Was it well between you? Some of you will not be able to believe that I am bringing this up. Don't I know what a cruel or mean person your father or mother was to you? What about all the hurts, the abandonment, the rejection, all the times you got hated or abused by your parent? What about them never being there for you or them even teaching you how to be a criminal. What about the example they set, shouldn't they be asking how their life is going and if it is well with them? If any of these are the kind of reactions you have when we begin to talk about your father, mother, or parent them I can guarantee that you need the healing truth of Jesus Christ in this very primary area of your life.

Bringing to remembrance what I said before, God has demonstrated that He is willing to love and accept people who have committed the worst sorts of crimes against others. Should it be any wonder then that this loving God who has called us to salvation and now calls us to grow up into the example and image of His Son Jesus wants us to face and deal with the past hurts in our lives caused by others? Should it be any wonder if He wants us to come to forgive them for what they have done? In fact this is God's path of cleansing us from the damage caused by these same hurts. This includes our parents just as well as anyone else.

It is one thing to be hurt by strangers but it is quite another to be hurt by those who should have loved you and protected you when you were young. The way of healing in this area is the same as for any other past hurts but it also starts to get us into the next area I am going to talk about which has to do with seeking forgiveness for the sins we have committed against others. We need to see our parents as God sees them, through Jesus Christ. Our parents are people also, they are sinners also and they also need the love and forgiveness of God to change their lives. Yes the hurt they gave us is very deep and personal, often very hard to forgive, but we must take those past hurts to the Lord, in the same way as I have already shown you in the last section, and work through them. Remember, work with God to find the root issue or deal with the things you already see and then ask God if there is more.

The second and very important part of this healing is to work with God to understand our own sin and iniquity regarding the relationships in the family or home we were born and or raised in. I have never seen this to be a one-way street. Through their sin the parents have brought damage and confusion to the children and we need to forgive them. Through their sin the children have turned around and brought damage and confusion to their relationship with their parents and we need to seek forgiveness for this.

In order to seek forgiveness from our parents we have to take our eyes off of what they did to us and look only at what was our responsibility to have done towards them. We also have to keep ourselves from justifying our bad behavior by weighing it against what they did to us. 'If they had raised me right I would not have been rebellious', that sort of thinking is a deception of the enemy and will not help you towards freedom. This is another area where you as an individual would need to work with the Lord in prayer to identify the nature of your sins as a young person who should have lived honestly and respectfully towards your parents, as much as it was possible on your part. Did you lie to your parents? Were you rebellious? Have you followed a path that disrespects them or the name they gave to you? Were you abusive to your parents in actions or language? Once you have identified and taken responsibility before God for these things, letting the Holy Spirit bring your heart to repentance, then you are ready to make that phone call or write that letter to communicate with your parent or parents. If you don't know where you can call or write then I would encourage you to write the letter anyway, in order to complete your thoughts and get it out of yourself for your own healing. Then send it to a friend or family member, keep it or destroy it. If your parents are no longer alive then through prayer tell God about your repentance and ask God to deliver the message to your parent or parents. In keeping with the teachings of the Bible, we should never try to communicate directly with the dead but God will know how to take care of what you tell Him.

What if you contact your parents and they don't accept you? What if they choose to be hard hearted and do not want anything more to do with you? Please understand that this is about breaking free from your cycle of slavery to sin not theirs. If your repentance touches them to respond with repentance of their own then praise God! If it does not then you have still done what needed to be done and are now free from that bondage. God will bless you and you will have more of the ease and peace of Jesus in your life. Remember the love of the Lord expressed towards us in Psalm 27:10 "When my father and my mother forsake me, Then the LORD will take care of me."

In my own case I was very blessed. My father and mother still live and I first heard this message when I was about 26. I went to both of my parents and found that they were more than happy to forgive and reconcile with me. The work of building real relationships started after that when the sin of my rebellion was no longer blocking the way.

After we have repented of dishonoring and sinning against our parents then we are ready to get back to honoring them. Honoring our parents or honoring the memory of our parents will take different forms for each person. Some of us have parents who are easier to honor than others. Some of us will have to look past their failures, possibly drug addiction or alcoholism or other bad behavior, to see the person God wanted them to be and simply honor the fact that God gave you life through them and somehow intended to use your relation with them in a positive way. This is an area where you may need more direction from the Holy Spirit but there are also some basics involved. We honor our parents when we are honest with them. We honor our parents when we keep ourselves from evil. We honor our parents when we are kind to them or speak kindly of them or of their memory. None of these last things I mentioned have anything to do with what kind of person they are, only with what kind of person we are.

Chapter Nine

The Forgotten Part of Forgiveness.

The forgotten part of forgiveness! Yes there is a large part of the forgiveness that the truth of Jesus has brought to us which often gets overlooked, possibly because it is the hardest part. We started to look at it in honoring our father and mother.

There are really three main parts to forgiveness. First we have the forgiveness of God who has decided that He will forgive the sin, trespass, transgression, and iniquity of anyone who will humbly come and receive the work that God's Son Jesus Christ has done for us through His death, burial, and resurrection. We are forgiven by God at that point and set free from the curse of eternal death and torment that was to be the payment for our sins.

Second, it is clear that we are to forgive others (including God) and ourselves. We have been working through the difficult parts of that through dealing with past hurts. In Matthew 6:15 the Lord Jesus makes it clear that God expects us to forgive, "But if you do not forgive men their trespasses, neither will your Father forgive your trespasses." Un-forgiveness of the sins of others keeps us in spiritual bondage and affects our lives with bitterness, anger, and other sins.

The third and mainly forgotten part of forgiveness is for us to go to those we have sinned against and seek forgiveness from them. If you have no problem with doing this then I salute you, but for most of us, until we learn this humility, this is one of the hardest things to do. Humility is probably the main reason that this can be so hard. It is one thing to humble your self to the God of the universe who has already promised to forgive. It is quite another thing to humble your self to another man or woman who may or may not choose to forgive. This can even be harder than going to one's parents. The main thing we need to remember is that Jesus would have us seek forgiveness from those we have wronged. If they are dead or cannot be found then we can tell God of our desire to be forgiven and ask Him to give them the message if they are dead or, if they live, to allow us to connect with them if it is His will that we should meet again. Our responsibility is to be honest about what we did. If the other person cannot accept this and forgive that is not our responsibility and they will have to answer to God for their part. In most cases we may be the only example of the humility of forgiveness they will ever see in their lifetime. Maybe God will use that in their life to draw them to Himself and help them begin to change. What is really going on here is that Jesus sees you every day and He also sees all the people that you have mistreated, lied to, stole from, or hurt in some way. We are as children to God and being a good Father if He can bring two of His children together when one has wronged the other then He will want the sinner to humbly apologize so that the hope of family relationships can be restored. Sin will be defeated. The one who humbles their self will be freed and blessed even if the other stays angry. James 4:10 reads, "Humble yourselves in the sight of the Lord, and He will lift you up."

The other part of seeking forgiveness from people we have wronged is to make restitution whenever possible, restitution is a big word that means to pay them back. Many times just the humility of coming to someone for forgiveness is the payback. When we have dishonored someone then humbling our self through asking to be forgiven pays them back as best as possible for the dishonor. If the dishonor was private then the humbling should be private. If the dishonor was public then the humbling should be public. That's restitution. If the crime was about money or things we may be able to pay it back or we may not be able to depending on what God has given us. If we are able to pay back then we need to be honest and offer to do so with willingness that if they say yes we will do it. God will expect this of us if we are able. The Old Testament gives specific instructions for restitution or payback. For simple stealing it was the original amount plus 20 percent. One of the main commandments is found in Numbers 5:5-7, "Then the LORD spoke to Moses, saying, 'Speak to the children of Israel: "When a man or woman commits any sin that men commit in unfaithfulness against the LORD, and that person is guilty, then he shall confess the sin which he has committed. He shall make restitution for his trespass in full, plus one-fifth of it, and give it to the one he has wronged."'" For animals (something most of us have never stolen) it was four to five times as much. In the New Testament we have the story of Zacchaeus from Luke 19:1-10. I will not quote it here, you can read it for yourself, but it clearly shows Jesus' great pleasure when this man was willing not only to repent but also to seek forgiveness and pay back those he had cheated. The people of the town were angry that Jesus went to be the guest of a sinner and then left their town but I can imagine their surprise the next day when the 'sinner' they hated so much started to go around and ask forgiveness for cheating them and even gave them back four times as much. Great healing came to Zacchaeus that day and a great opportunity for healing was given to the whole town of Jericho as well. I hope they took it.

For my own part the Lord showed me these principals during study of His word. I became convinced that it was the next thing He had for me to do. I made a list of the people I had wronged and asked God to help me make sure the list was complete. It took me three years to work through the list a little at a time. Some people I never found and had to give that over to God. Most people I was able to find and seek their forgiveness. For the most part it was well received and if I remember there was only one who would hear of my paying them back. When it was a store or business rather than a person I sent them the money with a letter of apology. I did learn not to press people about it just so I could 'feel good' about myself. There was one man who did not want to hear it and yet I felt bad so I called him again but it only offended him. I should have let that one go. In some cases God worked small miracles to help me find someone. One time I traveled to a river resort where I had stolen from a business as a youth. There had been a flood and this man's business was completely wiped out. I did not know who to ask about it but I saw a man sitting in a truck. I asked him and he told me that he was the owner and had lost everything in the flood. I told him why I was there. He even remembered the robbery from 15 or more years ago. I sought his forgiveness and gave him the money I had stolen plus 20 percent. He was very touched by God, he cried, thanked me, he was also a lover of Jesus and the money blessed him that day.

I cannot fully explain how following through on this part of forgiveness, and making restitution if possible, frees us from slavery to sin. Even if it did not we need to do this because it is right in the eyes of the Lord. It is His kindness expressed through us and shows His power through us to a world that, for the most part, does not know Him. But also it does bring freedom. I am far more released and at peace with both God and man because I went through this difficult part of healing my past. I cannot pay for my own sins, only Jesus can. But when there is someone I have wronged I owe them to make it as right as God allows me to do.

Chapter Ten

Repentance.

What is meant by repentance or to repent? As recorded in Matthew 4:17, "From that time Jesus began to preach and to say, 'Repent, for the kingdom of heaven is at hand.'" To repent simply means to turn. In other words, you were going this way, now turn around and go the other way. Those of us who have received Jesus as Lord and Savior have repented. We were living lives that were going on towards eternal death and have turned around and taken God's way instead which leads to eternal life. Now our need is to continue on in this repentance so that our whole soul: mind, will, and emotions are changed from the evil patterns we had always followed before.

In Romans 12:2 Paul talks about renewal of the mind, "And do not be conformed to this world, but be transformed by the renewing of your mind, that you may prove what is that good and acceptable and perfect will of God." This transformation happens as we spend the time and the years needed to learn the Word of God and the Ways of God through Bible study, through prayer, through serving God, and through our experiences as we let God work in our lives. You cannot be a lazy Christian and get your mind renewed and there are many things that you will never overcome in your life unless you get a renewed mind. At the same time that the Bible, prayer, service, and life experiences with God are renewing your mind they will also change your will and your emotions. A person seeking to learn about and serve God experiences change in their will over time. One of the main things that gets us into trouble is our desire to do what we want to do when we want to do it and how we want to do it. This rebellious will of our 'old man' or 'flesh' is in direct conflict to having a Lord and Master named Jesus who has His will for our lives. As we spend the time following and seeking Him our will and desire becomes to do His will. Jesus wrestled with this the night before He was arrested when He said in Matthew 26:39, "O My Father, if it is possible, let this cup pass from Me; nevertheless, not as I will, but as You will." Our emotions will even out over time as our minds receive His truth and our wills begin to desire what He wants. Oftentimes much of our emotional energy ends up spent on despair, depression, anger, feelings of worthlessness and failure. When we learn of and start choosing God's hope, love, acceptance of us as persons, and plan for our lives then many of the emotional struggles pass away.

You may also find that a number of the bad habits in your life can be broken through simple repentance. In other words, you see that the habit is wrong or bad for you so you go the other way. In most cases I suspect they will be tied to some decision or choice you have made. An example may be that I regularly over-eat and it is making me fat which is unhealthy for my body, the temple of God's Spirit. Why do I over-eat? For me it has been choices that I have made because I am unhappy. I feel unhappy so I comfort myself with food. I can spend time looking for the root of my unhappiness but at the same time I should try to repent, turn around, and go the other way by not over-eating. We should try to overcome bad habits through simple repentance. When we find out that this is not working then that is a clue that we should look deeper.

Repentance needs to be completed, whether we are simply turning away from something that is bad for us or if we have been delivered from a past hurt or emotional wound which has been with us for a long while. Always complete your repentance by filling with good the area of your life that was made clean. Jesus taught us the following concept in Luke 11:24-26, "When an unclean spirit goes out of a man, he goes through dry places, seeking rest; and finding none, he says, 'I will return to my house from which I came.' And when he comes, he finds it swept and put in order. Then he goes and takes with him seven other spirits more wicked than himself, and they enter and dwell there; and the last state of that man is worse than the first." While you may or may not be dealing with an evil spirit when you gain healing or freedom from a sin in your life the idea is the same. If all we do is clean out the bad but we don't change the way we live then we are leaving ourselves open to a future attack or future fall back into sin that can be worse than the first time around. When I come to the place where I forgive those who did me wrong and hurt me in the past I am letting go of my anger, hatred, and bitterness towards them. This will be a very freeing and cleansing experience from God. But, if after I am clean, I don't make any changes but rather I continue to allow myself to have the options of anger, hatred, bitterness towards the next person who comes along and offends me then I am setting myself up for another fall.

David the shepherd boy who became king of Israel in the Old Testament was declared by God to be a man after God's own heart. David also had his troubles and even fell into the gross sin of adultery and murder to cover it up. Those things were not what God wanted and David went through a period of denial. God was able to reach David's heart with conviction of sin and at that point we see from David a heart or spirit of repentance. We also need to develop a spirit of repentance that gives God control of where our lives are going to go, how they are going to develop, and who is going to be in control. Psalm 51 contains David's prayer of crisis repentance and it shows us what a repentant spirit is like, I record only verses 1 and 2 here: "Have mercy upon me, O God, According to Your lovingkindness; According to the multitude of Your tender mercies, Blot out my transgressions. Wash me thoroughly from my iniquity, And cleanse me from my sin." In Psalm 139:23-24, also written by David, we see what may be a more regular request of a man with a spirit of ongoing repentance, "Search me, O God, and know my heart; Try me, and know my anxieties; And see if there is any wicked way in me, And lead me in the way everlasting." In speaking of how Jesus was gaining more followers than himself John the Baptist put it like this in John 3:30 "He must increase, but I must decrease." This attitude of John is necessary for all who would live in a spirit of ongoing repentance that stays open to God.

Chapter Eleven

Dealing with Guilt.

All of us deal with that thing called guilt at some point in our lives. I recently went through what was for me a very great cleansing from guilt. It just seemed to build up over time and start to clog up my life. I was to the point of being really depressed because of the feelings of failure I was having. I have a large family and most of my children are now teenagers or young adults. That age group goes through a lot of changes whether we want them to or not and I was falling back on feelings of failure. Had I only spent more time with that one or done this with this one and so forth.

Now with guilt and overwhelming feelings of failure there can be either false guilt or true guilt or some mixture of the two. False guilt is where we spend time dwelling on ourselves as a failure and holding a pity party, poor me I'm a failure. This can only lead to one end, which will be depression and low self-esteem. To the extent that we let it continue, some let it go for years, it brings us into bondage and will affect our daily lives. This is not the truth of Jesus for us, it is not God's way. True guilt involves taking a real look at what is going on and always leads to repentance. In 2 Corinthians Paul had written to the Corinthian church about some things that were not right among them, a man among them had taken his own father's wife. The Corinthians repented, putting that man out of their fellowship and later offering to restore him when he repented. In this portion of scripture Paul talks about godly sorrow or true guilt, which leads to repentance. 2 Corinthians 7:8-12, "Now I rejoice, not that you were made sorry, but that your sorrow led to repentance. For you were made sorry in a godly manner, that you might suffer loss from us in nothing. For godly sorrow produces repentance leading to salvation, not to be regretted; but the sorrow of the world produces death. For observe this very thing, that you sorrowed in a godly manner: What diligence it produced in you, what clearing of yourselves, what indignation, what fear, what vehement desire, what zeal, what vindication! In all things you proved yourselves to be clear in this matter." Notice that the 'sorrow of the world', false guilt, brings death. It is death to walk around in a pity party all depressed and down on our selves for failure. It is life to let true guilt or godly sorrow lead us to repentance.

Once we have sorted out our guilty feelings, letting the true guilt show through, we are ready to work with God on repentance. Spend the time with God in prayer to get a sense of what you did or said or what you did not do or say. Seek His forgiveness and He will cleanse you. 1 John 1:9 "If we confess our sins, He is faithful and just to forgive us our sins and to cleanse us from all unrighteousness." Did your actions or words hurt or negatively affect someone else? Spend the time with God to see what should be done to make it as right as it can be made, apology, restitution. Once you have taken these steps in honesty then walk free from the guilt. You have been cleansed, forgiven, and set free by Jesus Christ Himself. It may be proper to still be ashamed of having failed or sinned in that way but it is improper to continue in depression and self-pity once we have worked it through honestly with God. Is there anything to big for Him to forgive and cleanse us from? Look at some of the examples in 1 Corinthians 6:9-11, "Do you not know that the unrighteous will not inherit the kingdom of God? Do not be deceived. Neither fornicators, nor idolaters, nor adulterers, nor homosexuals, nor sodomites, nor thieves, nor covetous, nor drunkards, nor revilers, nor extortioners will inherit the kingdom of God. And such were some of you. But you were washed, but you were sanctified, but you were justified in the name of the Lord Jesus and by the Spirit of our God." No there is nothing so big or that you are so guilty of that God will not deliver you from it through true guilt and honest repentance. That's the fullness of the power and purpose of Jesus Christ.

Chapter Twelve

Breaking Strongholds.

When Adam and Eve made the choice to disobey God's commandment in the Garden of Eden they fell away from God and into sin. They became sinners and their sin of disobedience passed on to all of us. Romans 5:12, "Therefore, just as through one man sin entered the world, and death through sin, and thus death spread to all men, because all sinned". But more happened on that day than immediately meets the eye. God had given Adam and Eve dominion over the earth. Genesis 1:27-28, "So God created man in His own image; in the image of God He created him; male and female He created them. Then God blessed them, and God said to them, 'Be fruitful and multiply; fill the earth and subdue it; have dominion over the fish of the sea, over the birds of the air, and over every living thing that moves on the earth.'" They were supposed to rule the earth for the good of man and the creatures. As members of God's camp they had been given responsibility and legal rights. Now the camp of the enemy came into the picture, the devil and his angels who are disobeyers of God. The devil tempted Eve and then Adam was tempted. They both chose to leave God's camp and join those who disobey God. With that choice they gave up their right to eternal life (they died spiritually) and their right to dominion and rule over the earth.

Thousands of years later when the devil would approach Jesus the Son of God to tempt Him to commit sin (to join those who disobey God) we hear him use these words in Luke 4:5-7, "Then the devil, taking Him up on a high mountain, showed Him all the kingdoms of the world in a moment of time. And the devil said to Him, 'All this authority I will give You, and their glory; for this has been delivered to me, and I give it to whomever I wish. Therefore, if You will worship before me, all will be Yours.'" Notice that in the verses following these Jesus rejects this temptation but also does not argue about the truth of the statement. Legal right to the kingdoms of the world and authority over the world had indeed been transferred from Adam and Eve to the devil when they sinned. This authority had been 'delivered' to the devil and he could give it to whomever he wished. Thanks be to God that after Jesus had completed the whole will of God the Father, had died on the cross for our sins, had been buried, and had risen from the dead, He was able to state in Matthew 28:18, "All authority has been given to Me in heaven and on earth." Jesus took back the rule and authority over the earth, which had been originally entrusted to Adam and Eve but which the devil had gained through their having joined him. Now how does that affect us? Often we too give over or have given over our rights to the enemy. He is able to say 'this has been delivered to me' and he has a right to keep us in bondage because we gave it to him. In the next few paragraphs I will cover a number of subjects that are related to this concept and which we will often find keeping us in slavery to sin if we have not yet dealt with them.

The first and foremost means of the devil gaining a stronghold over your life is if you have ever or continue to worship him or have practiced or continue to practice forms of witchcraft. From 2 Corinthians 6:14-16 we read: "Do not be unequally yoked together with unbelievers. For what fellowship has righteousness with lawlessness? And what communion has light with darkness? And what accord has Christ with Belial? Or what part has a believer with an unbeliever? And what agreement has the temple of God with idols? For you are the temple of the living God." We cannot be servants of God and servants of the devil at the same time. If you are going to be freed by the Son of God then you need to renounce all of your worship, obedience, and works that are involved directly with Satan or with any other religion or religious practice. Do not be deceived, all of man's religions in some form claim to be another way rather than the way God has provided through Christ. Even some forms of Christianity have been turned into no more than religious systems of traditions and works rather than of a relationship of salvation with Christ. You and I cannot be on two paths at the same time. We either choose God's way Jesus or we choose something else which is not His way even though it may have some or a lot of 'Jesus' mixed in. Now the word renounce means: to refuse to follow any further. You may have to spend some time with God to review your past and remember with Him if you have been involved in devil worship, witchcraft, or practice of false religions. Looking to Horoscopes, visiting a psychic or witch, seeking counsel from tarot or ouija boards, dowsing, all fall under witchcraft because you are looking for spiritual guidance from a source outside of God. We see from the ministry of Jesus as He cast out evil spirits from people that there are many evil spirits at work in the world. The angels who followed Satan are among us as demon spirits today and are not to be taken or interacted with lightly. Healing from this sort of spiritual bondage or connection to the devil or evil spirits is done through identifying the sin and any spirit involved, renouncing the sin and any spirit involved, seeking God's forgiveness for the sin, and asking God to cleanse you from the effects of the sin and fill you with His Spirit instead. I recommend that a person spend the time with God in prayer to do a thorough review of their life in regards to these things because the devil will use against you whatever he still has a right to use against you.

We can also bring ourselves into a form of spiritual bondage by some of the life decisions we make through vows, curses, and believed lies. These things then become a stronghold in our lives blocking our progress in Christ. It is even possible to be affected by the curses of others if we receive them and believe them. As an example, low self-esteem can keep Christians from finding and attaining their full potential in the life God has given to them. One of the most common ways that low self-esteem enters a person is when one of our parents or some other important adult figure in our life tells us that 'we are no good' or 'you will never amount to anything'. This is a curse that has been spoken on that child by someone who God put in authority over him or her. A young child rarely has the spiritual depth to reject such a lie and so we can internalize these things and start believing that 'I am no good', ' I will never amount to anything'. We accept the curse and turn around and curse ourselves. This can affect a person's whole life. Probably the best example of a vow from my own life was when my father told me he would not be coming home anymore. At that point I was very hurt but since I believed in the general lie that men and boys don't show their emotions, I made a vow, 'I'll never let anyone hurt me (emotionally) again'. Among other things this vow kept me from learning healthy expression of my emotions and from deep relationships with other people. Needless to say this has affected my married life over the years and I still have to work at emotional expression today because although I was healed I did not build up the normal years of experience in healthy expression of my emotions. This is an area where you will also need to spend some time with God to reveal any vows, self-curses, or believed lies that may still be affecting your life in a negative way. If you are aware of these things then the Holy Spirit is also more free to show you where or how you may be affected by them. The bottom line on vows is: don't! Jesus clearly taught us not to vow or make oaths (swearing that we would or would not do something). In Matthew 5:33-37 he said: "Again you have heard that it was said to those of old, 'You shall not swear falsely, but shall perform your oaths to the Lord.' "But I say to you, do not swear at all: neither by heaven, for it is God's throne; nor by the earth, for it is His footstool; nor by Jerusalem, for it is the city of the great King. Nor shall you swear by your head, because you cannot make one hair white or black. But let your 'Yes' be 'Yes,' and your 'No,' 'No.' For whatever is more than these is from the evil one.""

In dealing with vows or curses we have made or lies we have believed our greatest weapon is the truth of Jesus Christ. For vows we need to work with God in prayer to identify why we made that decision. Why did I declare that 'I'll never let anyone hurt me (emotionally) again'? When I got honest with the truth of Christ it was because I was very hurt and scared by the prospect of my father leaving the family. I was also trained in a lie that says that boys don't show their feelings. Talking to God about how

I felt, forgiving my father for leaving, accepting the truth that men and boys have emotions, which need healthy expression. Those are some of the steps I had to take with God to gain freedom from that vow.

Curses can take two forms: in one I have cursed someone else and need to repent of having done so for my own forgiveness and take my curse off of them. God's children are not supposed to be cursing others, James 3:10 reads, "Out of the same mouth proceed blessing and cursing. My brethren, these things ought not to be so." Cursing someone with words like 'go to hell' or 'rot in hell' is a grievous sin and needs to be repented. Telling your children they are 'no good' or 'you'll never amount to anything' can enter their heart and bind up their lives if they believe it. Why shouldn't they believe it? It came from their parent who deep down they know they should be able to trust. If I did so in secret then I can repent before God alone. If the person heard me then if possible I should contact them and ask their forgiveness as well. The second form of curses are the ones that people have put on us. I have already spoken about this earlier. Actually someone else can curse away all day and it will not affect me unless I receive it and believe it as the truth. As Christians, especially new Christians, we are in the process of gaining our understanding of the sure foundation that Jesus Christ has given us. We have been created by God on purpose, our lives are not an accident, (even if a parent tells us so), Jesus gave His very life to redeem me from sin so I am obviously of great value to God whether I feel like it or not. Building up and strengthening this foundation in our lives comes once again from getting into the truth of Jesus from the Bible, prayer, and serving God. As we learn who God is, who we are in Him, what His plan and purpose is for our lives, we become as Ephesians 6:10 says, "...strong in the Lord and in the power of His might." People will no longer be able to feed us lies about ourselves because we know the truth about ourselves. As you are learning of God you may run into 'lies' that you have believed. Perhaps you were told that your birth was just an accident but now you read Psalm 139, which tells you that God planned for you to be. Renounce that lie in prayer, reject it and pray receiving the truth of God in it's place.

Chapter Thirteen

Freedom from Sexual Bondage.

Another area where we can find ourselves in bondage is captivity through sexual bonding. Now I will be using the example of marriage to bring out the fullness of this teaching. Those of you who have never been married please have patience and read on, this section will apply to you as well. We are very clearly taught that God's plan was for one man to have one woman, and vice versa, until death do us part, (see Matthew 19:1-10 as an example). After the death of our spouse we are free to marry again. Now I am not going to spend my time arguing here about divorce and remarriage and whether it is right or wrong. I think we all might agree that with the divorce rate running about 50% in our country, (even among Christians), that there is something wrong and that people are treating their marriages much more lightly than God would have them do so. The Bible clearly teaches that God hates divorce, (Malachi 2:13-16). God has shown Himself to be a God of reconciliation through Christ, bringing all things together. Surely, if we believe that God can do anything then we have to allow that He can heal our marriages. Instead of considering divorce we should work through our part to break the cycles of sin in our lives and pray that our spouse will do the same. Divorce does however happen to Christians, either through their own fault or being left by spouses who don't choose to continue. Some of them don't choose to continue because we are so busy doing things that drive them away. If the fault is yours it can be worked through with God and proper repentance and restitution made as for any other sin. For more information on this subject read 1 Corinthians 7:10-16. Enough about divorce I was going to talk about sexual bondage.

Assuming that we have that one wife or one husband, as God intended, we would find ourselves pictured by the words which Adam spoke in one of the very first prophecies in Genesis 2:24, "Therefore a man shall leave his father and mother and be joined to his wife, and they shall become one flesh." Jesus reaffirmed this in Matthew 19:5 adding in verse 6, "So then, they are no longer two but one flesh." There is obviously supposed to be something very special about that relationship where we are no longer two but one. There is more happening than just a description of the sexual act, becoming one flesh. Actually a husband and wife are joined in their souls in an unseen way. What the one does and chooses affects the other much more directly than it affects anyone outside the marriage. There is a sense of either healthy belonging to each other and no one else or there is an unhealthy sense of ownership, 'I own you and no one else does'. Looking further into this 'bond' that takes place with a sexual mate we read in 1 Corinthians 6:15-17, "Do you not know that your bodies are members of Christ? Shall I then take the members of Christ and make them members of a harlot? Certainly not! Or do you not know that he who is joined to a harlot is one body with her? For 'the two,' He says, 'shall become one flesh.' But he who is joined to the Lord is one spirit with Him." These verses indicate that when we have improper sexual relations outside of marriage that the same one flesh 'bond' happens as does inside of a marriage. Another passage of scripture that would indicate that there is some sort of unholy bond or hold on us from sexual relations outside of marriage is Proverbs Chapter 5. Because of it's length I will not reprint it completely here but the whole chapter is a warning from father to son to avoid those who are sexually immoral, verses 9-12 "Lest you give your honor to others, And your years to the cruel one; Lest aliens be filled with your wealth, And your labors go to the house of a foreigner; And you mourn at last, When your flesh and your body are consumed, And say: 'How I have hated instruction, And my heart despised correction!'" Somehow we will pay if we join ourselves in sexual immorality. The effects of sexually transmitted disease may also be suggested by the above passage. In the book of Romans 1:18 we read "For the wrath of God is revealed from heaven against all ungodliness and unrighteousness of men, who suppress the truth in unrighteousness". The chapter goes on to list what suppressing the truth in unrighteousness means including sexual immorality, Romans 1:24-27, "Therefore God also gave them up to uncleanness, in the lusts of their hearts, to dishonor their bodies among themselves, who exchanged the truth of God for the lie, and worshiped and served the creature rather than the Creator, who is blessed forever. Amen. For this reason God gave them up to vile passions. For even their women exchanged the natural use for what is against nature. Likewise also the men, leaving the natural use of the woman, burned in their lust for one another, men with men committing what is shameful, and receiving in themselves the penalty of their error which was due." As it states there is a penalty to be received for such actions.

Now as Christians we should have nothing to do with these things any longer. 1 Corinthians 6:18-20 reads "Flee sexual immorality. Every sin that a man does is outside the body, but he who commits sexual immorality sins against his own body. Or do you not know that your body is the temple of the Holy Spirit who is in you, whom you have from God, and you are not your own? For you were bought at a price; therefore glorify God in your body and in your spirit, which are God's." This passage also clearly indicates that sexual immorality is different from other sins because it is a sin against our own body.

Where does this leave us as Christians? Many of us have walked in sexual immorality even after coming to Christ. First I want to address some of the ways we got to this place where we were willing to sin against our own body and then I will talk about what we can do about it to walk away clean in the Lord.

One of the main ways we get into sexual immorality in the first place is through following the crowd, peer pressure from our friends, or just believing that everybody does it. From these we make soft choices, which end up having an effect on our future and on our ability to live unconfused lives. Another main way we get into sexual immorality is through abuse. I know that abuse is one of the hidden sins of American families. More of it goes on than any of us would like to admit. Children are often emotionally abused and made to feel worthless which drives them to forms of self-punishment, like allowing others to use or abuse them sexually. Children are also forced into sexual acts by family members or friends of family more often than by strangers. You may have heard of the term 'lost innocence', in a large part that is what happens when we either begin to let ourselves practice sexual immorality or when it is forced upon us. In the first case we let down our guard and begin sinning against God's ways and our own body, which is bad enough and starts a lust or drive or iniquity in our hearts to have more improper sexual pleasure. Often this in itself will lead to situations where we end up getting used and abused sexually. In the second case being forced sexually breaks down our natural God given child-like ability to trust people. In both cases we end up bonding with the partner or the one who forced us as the line is crossed regarding God's 'the two shall become one flesh' principal. To further complicate the picture an abused person can either become sexually dysfunctional which can lead to problems with having relationships in future marriage or they can become abusers of themselves who prostitute their bodies. Those who abuse themselves in this way are often trying to punish themselves because of feelings of worthlessness or low self-esteem. Reviewing again the case of the prisoner I mentioned earlier, who had recently come to Christ but was also a prison prostitute, giving his body to other men. He wanted to know what to do as he now believed that this was against God but felt helpless to stop (driven by iniquity). We looked together at how his self-abuse was a reaction to being homosexually raped as a child. He was still extremely angry with his first abusers. I pointed out that the start of his path of freedom (from the drive of this iniquity) lay in realizing how much he had been forgiven by Jesus and being able to then freely forgive those who had started this abuse in him. Sometimes you may find yourself needing this kind of work by the Holy Spirit before you can be free from continuing a pattern of sexual immorality. Be honest with yourself in this area. Don't deceive yourself, using an assumption about hidden iniquity (God hasn't shown me yet) as an excuse to continue.

As a side note here, if you have been a rapist, molester, or someone who has forced yourself on children or others then know that you have caused great damage to their souls. The path of freedom for you includes getting in touch with God on this, repenting, hopefully grieving such sin in godly sorrow, and whatever confession and apology God makes possible towards those you have hurt. Certainly if you were a parent or adult family member you need to try and make direct repentance to the younger family member you hurt. It is probably still affecting their life today.

Now regarding any past sexual immorality, whether done through your will or forced through abuse, we want to take the opportunity in Christ to walk away free and clean from any entrapment of our soul or hold these things may still have on us through improper bonding or lies we have believed. We also want to reset our hearts and minds with God's truth about proper sexual behavior and reject the world's twisted lies about what is OK. Those lies are hurting a lot of people. We need to learn and hold onto the truths of God's word the Bible because God does not change who He is or what He has said just because the world says 'hey we are living in modern times don't you know?' People are still going to be judged by God's standards and in those standards sexual enjoyment and fulfillment, which God intended for the whole person: spirit, soul, and body, not just for satisfying the body, is found in the committed relationship of marriage. Extra-marital sexual relations are still a sin and have no place for someone following Christ. This goes for homosexuality, lesbianism, adultery, bestiality and any other perversion of God's naturally created order. Let's remember that although God knows about the past sins and any perversions we have walked in He has forgiven us if we have been saved through Jesus Christ. We are now washed and sanctified, set apart for God, in Christ and are not going to be judged for things done in the past. The aim here is not to get clean for salvation, we already have that, but rather to gain freedom for our souls, break any possible future patterns and help ourselves to more easily obey the Lord's word to 'flee sexual immorality'.

Breaking the bonds of past improper sexual relations you may have had is similar to working through any other group of past sins. If you are committed to doing a complete job of clean up then you will have to spend time with God in prayer asking Him to bring what you did back to memory. These things should be examined for what they are and worked through one at a time breaking each 'one flesh' bond that you have made. If you are not convinced that something God brings to memory was really a sin then be honest and ask Him to reveal to you what was wrong with it. Once you know the sin confess what you did and ask God to forgive you, (1 John 1:9). Renounce the bonding of your soul to that other person, 'Father God I break the bond of one flesh that was made between myself and this person in Jesus name'. Ask the Holy Spirit to come and cleanse and fill that area of your soul with Himself. Purpose in your heart that you will not walk in those ways again and ask God for the power not to do so, (2 Timothy 1:7). If the act you were involved in was an act of abuse that you did to someone else then seek God's forgiveness for having hurt that person and having brought fear and mistrust to their lives, then ask God what you can do to make it right. Would he have you call them? Write a letter? Sometimes these things are not possible but often they are and remember, God still sees both you and them every day. If the act was forced upon you then work with God to come to terms of forgiveness for the person or persons who violated you and broke your trust. Remember that we cannot have true freedom with a God who has forgiven us everything if we are going to continue to hold the people who wronged us by the neck of un-forgiveness insisting that they pay us what they owe. You may have to renounce the fear and mistrust that came into your life at that time. God bless you as you deal with this very difficult area of life in Christ. I will say that if you have been the victim of sexual abuse you have probably been deeply wounded. I have known such people whose heart and mind work overtime to protect them from relationships because of the overwhelming spirit of fear that entered them at the time of abuse. Please consider this because it can become very controlling of what you will or will not do in your life and tends to block out your ability to follow the Lord's way. Keep seeking Jesus on this and He will show you the way out. It is not that the way out of this kind of wounding is much different or harder than other recovery, it is that our own heart and mind, filled with fears, work against us to recover from sexual abuse. Maybe this is what is meant when the word says, "Every sin that a man does is outside the body, but he who commits sexual immorality sins against his own body", (1 Corinthians 6:18).

Chapter Fourteen

Dealing with the Devil.

1 Peter 5:7-9, "Be sober, be vigilant; because your adversary the devil walks about like a roaring lion, seeking whom he may devour. Resist him, steadfast in the faith, knowing that the same sufferings are experienced by your brotherhood in the world." This passage from First Peter states it very clearly, we have an adversary and enemy of those who love and follow Jesus and it is the devil. The devil or Satan or Lucifer is a person of some mystery in the Bible. God's word gives us some insight that leads us to believe he was one of the head angels but chose to rebel against God. For this he and the angels who followed him were cast from heaven to earth. Jesus confronted these fallen angels, now called demons, as we read about Jesus casting out demons or evil spirits in the gospel books of Matthew, Mark, Luke, and John. We read references about the devil and hear about his undermining work throughout the Bible. We know from the book of Job chapter 1:6-12 that the devil is not just a free agent doing whatever he pleases but rather he must

get permission from God and is really only able to do what God allows him to do. Far from being the 'king' of hell the devil knows that his time is short (Revelation 12:12), and that he will be cast into the lake of fire and brimstone and be tormented day and night forever and ever (Revelation 20:10). As I pointed out before, the devil is able to rule over those areas that have been legally given to him as Adam gave over his rights as master of the world. Why does God allow such a person to exist? We are not told. It seems that he is still a part of what God is allowing to happen in this fallen world as God keeps mankind responsible for our choices and also seeks for those who are still lost. We also know that Jesus gave his followers authority "…over all the power of the enemy…" (Luke 10:19), and to drive out evil spirits, "And these signs will follow those who believe: In My name they will cast out demons…" (Mark 16:17).

Probably the most important thing we need to know about this enemy of the faith is how he operates. How does he deceive people and work out his will? How do we recognize him at work in our lives and our world? A large part of the answer to this is contained in the Old Testament passage of Isaiah 14:12-15 which clearly talks about the devil, using his name Lucifer, and shows us what kind of spirit he really is: "How you are fallen from heaven, O Lucifer, son of the morning! How you are cut down to the ground, you who weakened the nations! For you have said in your heart: 'I will ascend into heaven, I will exalt my throne above the stars of God; I will also sit on the mount of the congregation On the farthest sides of the north; I will ascend above the heights of the clouds, I will be like the Most High.' Yet you shall be brought down to Sheol, to the lowest depths of the Pit." Listen to the statements the devil made and purposed in his heart: five times he declares 'I will'! This then is the nature and spirit of the devil, that self centered spirit that does not seek the Lord's will but it's own will. This is the same sin nature of our 'flesh' that passed on to us when Adam and Eve chose their own will instead of God's. This is where the created one gets worshipped rather than the creator. Now that we know this we can much more easily see how the devil and even our own fleshly nature work to deceive us. We need to be careful to admit that it is not just 'the devil made me do it'. The Bible clearly states in Jeremiah 17:9, "The heart is deceitful above all things, and desperately wicked; who can know it?" In James 1:14 we learn that our own desires are what get used when we are tempted, "But each one is tempted when he is drawn away by his own desires and enticed." So we can recognize the work and plans that the devil has against us by the presence of a spirit of self or selfishness. This will often be a combination of suggestions in our mind and our own evil desires that play on iniquity we have not yet worked through with God. It is written of the devil that he "...transforms himself into an angel of light", (read 2 Corinthians 11:13-15). No wonder then that he does not introduce himself, 'hello I am the devil and I want you to do something against God'. Rather he uses the disguise of self with the thoughts he brings to us being as if they were our own ideas. If these ideas play on some area where we have not dealt with our sin then we can easily fall into this trap. This is especially true for those who have received Jesus as Savior but have not committed their own lives to him as Lord. If you are still living on your own terms and in your own will instead of God's then you are an easy tool for the devil to use. Also those who have or are following one or more of the popular self-realization religions like New Age or Buddhism will find themselves easily deceived since self and self-centeredness is one of the main attacks of the enemy. The only sure defense is to be committed to God's will as Jesus gave us example. Then as a person of prayer who is coming to know God better, as someone who spends time in the word to know God's will, as someone who is dealing with their past rather than ignoring it, you will not be easily deceived into sin.

The Bible teaches us how to win the war against our enemy the devil. There are a number of fields in this battle, which I will cover: resistance, spiritual warfare, and dealing with temptation.

Resistance

In the passage from 1 Peter 5 that we started this section with and in the book of James we are told to resist the devil and are given the assurance that it will work. James 4:7, "Therefore submit to God. Resist the devil and he will flee from you." Although spiritual warfare and dealing with temptation are also ways to resist the devil the most simple and straightforward way of resistance is to tell him 'no'. If we recognize that something is being suggested in our minds that we know is not right then we have a choice to make. Will we do it or not do it? Basically the devil is saying this is my way you will like it, come this way. Our response is 'no' I am going to chose God's way instead. For example: you see someone who has treated you poorly in the past and your instant thought is to find a way to get even. You know this is the devil trying to find out if he can work on you to get you to take his path rather than God's. You know it to be wrong and reject this temptation for the sin that it is, knowing that God's word says in Romans 12:19-21 "Beloved, do not avenge yourselves, but rather give place to wrath; for it is written, 'Vengeance is Mine, I will repay,' says the Lord. Therefore 'If your enemy is hungry, feed him; If he is thirsty, give him a drink; for in so doing you will heap coals of fire on his head.' Do not be overcome by evil, but overcome evil with good."

Spiritual Warfare

Spiritual warfare is a way of turning the tables on our enemy the devil rather than just dealing with him when he messes with us. We read in Ephesians 6:10-18, "Finally, my brethren, be strong in the Lord and in the power of His might. Put on the whole armor of God, that you may be able to stand against the wiles of the devil. For we do not wrestle against flesh and blood, but against principalities, against powers, against the rulers of the darkness of this age, against spiritual hosts of wickedness in the heavenly places. Therefore take up the whole armor of God, that you may be able to withstand in the evil day, and having done all, to stand. Stand therefore, having girded your waist with truth, having put on the breastplate of righteousness, and having shod your feet with the preparation of the gospel of peace; above all, taking the shield of faith with which you will be able to quench all the fiery darts of the wicked one. And take the helmet of salvation, and the sword of the Spirit, which is the word of God; praying always with all prayer and supplication in the Spirit, being watchful to this end with all perseverance and supplication for all the saints".

There are definite times when spiritual warfare is needed. Many of the negative things that happen to us can have deeper causes than meet the eye. Difficulties in marriage and relationships that seem to be unsolvable, areas of little or no progress in life when we know that God wants us to do or be involved in that thing, perhaps unexplained sickness or disaster. There is a need to put our families and what God has given us under spiritual protection. There are also the times when we are stepping out to do the will of God. As the passage above says, 'we do not wrestle against flesh and blood'. Sometimes it is easier to see people as the problem, such as a husband or wife or children rather than to realize that often we have spiritual enemies to deal with. The passage also speaks of areas of principality and power and rulers of the darkness of this age. Any person or 'territory' that has been given over to the enemy through sin, through iniquity, through witchcraft or other evil can be subject to evil forces. During his ministry Jesus explained how he did spiritual warfare. In Matthew 12:28-29 we read Jesus words, "But if I cast out demons by the Spirit of God, surely the kingdom of God has come upon you. Or how can one enter a strong man's house and plunder his goods, unless he first binds the strong man? And then he will plunder his house." Jesus also declared for his people, recorded in Matthew 16:19, "And I will give you the keys of the kingdom of heaven, and whatever you bind on earth will be bound in heaven, and whatever you loose on earth will be loosed in heaven." The answer to Jesus' question is that you cannot enter a strong man's house and plunder his goods unless you first bind him. So we need to bind the enemy, whether it be the devil or some other evil spirit or power or principality that God shows to us, bind them through prayer in the name of Jesus, so that we can remove them from being a problem or hindrance any further in whatever area of life we are dealing with.

To do this effectively there are a couple of things we need to understand. The first and most important is that we should not enter spiritual warfare unless we are hearing from the Spirit of God to do so. This requires listening prayer and a commitment, once again, to God's plans and will rather than our own. There is a story in Acts 19:11-20 that shows us a comparison of Paul walking this out in God's will and the power which came as a result and some others who tried to do it in their will and the disaster it caused for them. If we ask the Lord to reveal to us if there are spiritual forces at work He can tell us. Then He can tell us what spirits we are up against and how to pray effectively and bind them. The next thing we need to know is that it is all about authority. If we understand how authority works then we will understand, as I have pointed out already, how the enemy got the power in the first place. Also if we understand authority then we can have confidence taking back from the enemy whatever God had intended to be under our authority. Do you know that God has given husbands authority over wives? Parents authority over their children? Employers authority in matters of work over employees? Leaders of ministry groups authority over those in them for matters of the ministry? If we are in one of these positions then we can exercise that authority with confidence against spiritual wickedness that would hinder or destroy those under us. (Remember we should never miss-use authority. God's plan is that leaders be servants not lords, Mark 10:45.) In the gospel of Matthew 8:5-13 we have the story of a Roman centurion who understood authority, it says that Jesus marveled at him because of this understanding and said to those nearby, "Assuredly, I say to you, I have not found such great faith, not even in Israel!" So faith, the shield of faith, which we use to 'quench all the fiery darts of the wicked one' is connected to understanding our God given authority. I have also had times when I knew that spiritual warfare needed to be done but I also knew that I was not the one in authority at the time. Some of these times Jesus has told me to pray the warfare bindings anyway (possibly because the person in authority was not listening to Him or did not know Him). At those times Jesus reminds me of Matthew 28:18, "And Jesus came and spoke to them, saying, 'All authority has been given to Me in heaven and on earth.'" Jesus can do this because He has all authority. From this I know that when He tells me to do so then I can pray against spiritual powers with confidence.

I would now like to give you an example of specific binding prayer, which I use some form of, in faith, depending on the situation, for spiritual warfare. Recently I was spending some time in prayer over a difficult relationship problem in my family. The Lord showed me that there was a spirit of fear keeping us from progress. I knew there was fear on my part. Fear of opening up, of risking my feelings in the relationship, of being rejected. I waited on how God would have me work this through and then I prayed in line with Ephesians chapter 6:10-18, 'Satan I bind you and every power and principality, every ruler of the darkness of this world, and every spiritual force of wickedness in the heavenly realm, all demons and every evil worker. I bind you in the name of Jesus. I break the power of the spirit of fear from off of myself and my family and I order you out of my life. Be rooted up and cast into the sea, I order you into the abyss. In the name of Jesus, amen! Father God I ask you in the name of Jesus to enforce this binding and to bring in your Holy Spirit to fill and cleanse this area of our lives.' As you can see I believe in pouring it on. The prayer may take different forms at times but once I understand what is going on I am not going to allow my enemy any place whatever. That is the attitude you have to have and God will give you the victory over them.

Dealing with Temptation

I have already mentioned the way the devil tempts us, through self-suggesting thoughts, trying to play on our weaknesses. I have also already written about how to say 'no' and go God's way instead. There are just a few more things I would like to say about dealing with temptation which I think need to be understood.

First, temptation is not sin. Of course a husband should probably not say to his wife or a man to his girlfriend 'honey I was tempted by that beautiful woman who just walked by'. I can guarantee that she will not likely understand or appreciate the difference between temptation and sin at that moment. Temptation does not become sin unless we say 'yes' to it and follow it or let it play in our minds. James 1:14-15 teaches this to us, "But each one is tempted when he is drawn away by his own desires and enticed. Then, when desire has conceived, it gives birth to sin; and sin, when it is full-grown, brings forth death." There is a progression from temptation, then if followed by desire to sin and then to death in that area of our lives. Everyone is tempted but we all chose to sin or not sin. Everyone? Yes even Jesus. Hebrews 4:14-15, "Seeing then that we have a great High Priest who has passed through the heavens, Jesus the Son of God, let us hold fast our confession. For we do not have a High Priest who cannot sympathize with our weaknesses, but was in all points tempted as we are, yet without sin." Jesus was tempted in all points just like you and me but He did not sin, temptation is not sin, choosing to follow the temptation leads to sin.

Secondly, Jesus has given us His example of how best to stand up against temptation. In Matthew 4:1-11 (also repeated in Luke 4:1-13) we read about Jesus' direct temptation from the enemy. This may be somewhat different from the more indirect ways the devil tempts us but the way Jesus took care of it, by quoting God's truth and standing by it (remember from Ephesians 6, the belt of truth and the sword of the Spirit which is the word of God) is still our example. As we spend time in the word

of God to know God's ways we will be able to stand up
for them as Jesus did. Let's notice how Jesus did this from
Matthew 4:1-11, "Then Jesus was led up by the Spirit into
the wilderness to be tempted by the devil. And when He
had fasted forty days and forty nights, afterward He was
hungry. Now when the tempter came to Him, he said,
'If You are the Son of God, command that these stones
become bread.' But He answered and said, 'It is written,
"Man shall not live by bread alone, but by every word
that proceeds from the mouth of God."' Then the devil
took Him up into the holy city, set Him on the pinnacle of
the temple, and said to Him, 'If You are the Son of God,
throw Yourself down. For it is written: "He shall give His
angels charge over you," and, "In their hands they shall
bear you up, Lest you dash your foot against a stone."'
Jesus said to him, 'It is written again, "You shall not tempt
the LORD your God."' Again, the devil took Him up
on an exceedingly high mountain, and showed Him all
the kingdoms of the world and their glory. And he said
to Him, 'All these things I will give You if You will fall
down and worship me.' Then Jesus said to him, 'Away
with you, Satan! For it is written, "You shall worship the
LORD your God, and Him only you shall serve."' Then the
devil left Him, and behold, angels came and ministered
to Him." (Notice how the devil tried using the word of
God to trick Jesus when he saw Jesus was going to deny
him by use of the word of God.)

Lastly in dealing with temptation we need to understand
that the pressure from the enemy is not necessarily going
to go away just because we say 'no' once. The word resist
can mean that we will have to resist for a while. We are
promised (James 4:7) that he, the devil, will flee if we resist
him. Other words that seem to show that we may have to
put up continuing resistance are found in the following
passages on temptation. Of Jesus in Hebrews 2:18, "For in

that He Himself has suffered, being tempted, He is able to aid those who are tempted." Suffered possibly indicates that it was not always a quick solution but that even Jesus had to resist for however long it took. In James 1:12 we read, "Blessed is the man who endures temptation; for when he has been approved, he will receive the crown of life which the Lord has promised to those who love Him." Again there is a word 'endures' that seems to say temptation can be hard to get through. Our comfort comes from God's promise to stand with us, 1 Corinthians 10:13, "No temptation has overtaken you except such as is common to man; but God is faithful, who will not allow you to be tempted beyond what you are able, but with the temptation will also make the way of escape, that you may be able to bear it."

One last area I would like address in dealing with the devil is when we are confronted by demon possession in other persons. Typically I would not expect demon possession in a Christian unless they have really backslidden from the Lord. But we might find it in someone, that is not a Christian or who has backslid, who is either under our ministry or family or authority or with whom we have to interact in some way. I do not personally have a lot of direct experience in this area so I want to limit what I say. I will say that the Lord can show us what we need to know. In the gospels Jesus even spoke to the demon(s) at times requiring it's or their name, (see His example in Mark 5:1-20). As with all things, once we know what we are dealing with we can then pray confidently and effectively for deliverance from the demon.

Chapter Fifteen

Controlling Behaviors.

Many of us have developed unhealthy behaviors related to either allowing others to control us or controlling others.

If we find that we are the type of person who lets the forcefulness, anger, or possible reaction of others control what we will or will not do or what we will or will not say then it is very possible that we do not have a good understanding or definition of who we are as a person. It is possible that we do not know where we begin and other people end. We don't know how to say 'no' because of our fears of the reactions of others. This is a form of the sin of idolatry because we are letting someone other than Jesus be 'Lord' in those areas of our lives. (This was a big problem for me personally.)

If we find that we are the type of person who uses forcefulness, anger, co-dependence, or other manipulation to get others to do what we want then it is very possible that we also do not have a good understanding or definition of who we are as a person. It is possible that we do not

know where we end and other people begin. We have
a hard time hearing 'no' from others and accepting that
things should not always go our way or that our ideas
should not always be accepted. In short we are insisting
on the place that the Lord should have in the lives of those
around us and this is sin.

How does a person end up with these kind of immature
responses to life? Usually these are formed when we
are little children and our parents or guardians lack of
guidance or overbearing guidance confused us and we
failed to develop healthy boundaries of who we are apart
from other people.

I am not going to try and explain all of this in detail, as I
don't feel that I am really qualified to do so. I will however
try to explain what I do know. A large part of growing up
in Christ and becoming mature Christians has to do with
knowing who we are and who we are not. This goes hand
in hand with understanding what is our responsibility
and what is not. When we know who we are in Christ
then we can more honestly take responsibility for our
own choices and actions and sins without blaming them
on or yielding them to someone else.

You and I are unique and special creations of God. We
are here both to learn of God and to "…grow in the grace
and knowledge of our Lord and Savior Jesus Christ…", (2
Peter 3:18). I will not stand at the judgment for your sins
and you will not stand at the judgment for my sins. I have
not been put here to be either lord over you or to yield to
you as lord any more than you have been put here to do
either of these for me.

Knowing more of who we are in Jesus Christ will help
us to define our own boundaries. Therefore the answer
for both of these problems is to continue to move forward
in your walk with God.

For those of us who have allowed others to rule over us in the place that should belong only to God, we need to confess this as sin, repent of our idolatry and work with God through our fears. In some cases we may have to avoid those who want to dominate us. It is important to seek God throughout this process, as He is really the only one who will know what to do. My suggestion is to start praying for the person(s) we have been subject to, as God wants to work in their life also.

For those of us who have used our power and forcefulness over others or co-depended for them, we need to see this for what it really is, repent and stop trying to take God's place in their lives. To be healthy we need to come to the point where we can respect other people as persons in their own right and not control and manipulate them to get what we want or fulfill their responsibilities for them when they could do so themselves. We may believe that we only want the best for someone else but keeping another person under control through the force of our personality is entirely selfish and anti-Christian behavior. Likewise, co-depending for other people and taking on their responsibilities for them enables them to continue in bad behavior and not grow up. The strange thing about co-dependents is that they 'seem' to want what is best for the other but it is still a form of selfishness, getting what they want. When we manipulate in this way because of what we think is right then we are not blessing the other person at all but rather keeping them from taking responsibility for their lives and from growing up in the Lord.

A healthy person knows who they are and develops God centered reasons for the things they say and do. They are free to choose to serve others for God's glory rather than just doing what they see as right or acting because they feel that they have to do so. In John 13:3-5 we see this example in Jesus Who definitely knew who He was, "Jesus, knowing that the Father had given all things into His hands, and that He had come from God and was going to God, rose from supper and laid aside His garments, took a towel and girded Himself. After that, He poured water into a basin and began to wash the disciples' feet, and to wipe them with the towel with which He was girded."

A healthy person can allow others to suffer for their mistakes or unwillingness to take action. This is how they will learn and when we refuse to let one of our children or someone important to us go through this learning we are enabling bad behavior in them. Parents should watch over their children and protect them. But parents who always rescue their child or a person who always rescues others when they mess up is not necessarily doing them a favor. Mark 10:17-22, "Now as He was going out on the road, one came running, knelt before Him, and asked Him, 'Good Teacher, what shall I do that I may inherit eternal life?' So Jesus said to him, 'Why do you call Me good? No one is good but One, that is, God. You know the commandments: "Do not commit adultery," "Do not murder," "Do not steal," "Do not bear false witness," "Do not defraud," "Honor your father and your mother."' And he answered and said to Him, 'Teacher, all these I have observed from my youth.' Then Jesus, looking at him, loved him, and said to him, 'One thing you lack: Go your way, sell whatever you have and give to the poor, and you will have treasure in heaven; and come, take up the cross, and follow Me.' But he was sad at this word, and went away sorrowful, for he had great possessions." Jesus loved this man and watched him go. He did not rescue him or prevent him from his choice.

If you recognize yourself to be either controlled, controlling or enabling in these ways then I encourage you to spend time with God in prayer to work on understanding who you are, what you are and are not responsible for, where you end or begin, and where others end and begin.

Chapter Sixteen

Your Body the Temple of God's Holy Spirit.

1 Corinthians 3:16-17, "Do you not know that you are the temple of God and that the Spirit of God dwells in you? If anyone defiles the temple of God, God will destroy him. For the temple of God is holy, which temple you are." 1 Corinthians 6:19-20, "Or do you not know that your body is the temple of the Holy Spirit who is in you, whom you have from God, and you are not your own? For you were bought at a price; therefore glorify God in your body and in your spirit, which are God's."

Our bodies are a gift from God and also a responsibility from Him. As Christians we understand from the Bible that God considers them to be the 'temple' of His Holy Spirit who entered us when we received Jesus as our Savior. In this chapter I just want to point out a few important things.

First, as much as is possible on our part, we are not to neglect our bodies with lack of: exercise, sleep, necessary food and drink, and general care so that they are as ready for the Lord's purposes as they can be. Second, that we should not over indulge ourselves in food, drink, medication (including drug use) or other things that would then be harmful to the body. It is all too easy for us to get into habits or even addictions that leave us tired or out of shape and not ready for our Master's work. Since our body, soul, and spirit are intimately connected within us there is an effect on the whole person when any one of these three is weak. For example, it is much easier and more of a delight to spend time renewing our mind in the word of God when our body is not tired or unnecessarily hungry. In most cases bad habits of caring for our bodies have entered in slowly. Sometimes there are reasons for these that we will have to seek the Lord to discover. As with other areas we have been covering, when we find ourselves in a bad habit that is affecting how we care for our body, the 'temple' of God, then try to change it and start a healthy habit to replace it. If this does not work then start bringing the situation to God in prayer to find out if there is a root cause that needs to be removed.

Drug and alcohol abuse is a very large topic. I have already shown from my own life that there are definite reasons why people end up addicted. Almost always the person is using the substance to hide from something they do not want to face up to about their self. Don't be deceived, if you are using drugs or alcohol even occasionally with any kind of idea like: 'it helps me fit in' or 'I find it easier to relate to people' then you are hiding who God made you to be rather than working with Him to find yourself. It is impossible to be an honest follower of Jesus, one who is being real with those around them, one who seeks God and does His will in this world, if you are stoned on drugs or drunk.

Regarding physical sickness, we see Jesus and the early disciples healing sickness through the laying on of hands and prayer and various other means. In our day and age the Lord has allowed mankind to gain much medical wisdom to the point where many diseases can be prevented and much suffering relieved. A small percentage of Christians believe that we should trust in prayer only, most go to the doctor when sick. The body belongs to God and is a part of the whole person: body, soul, and spirit. Therefore as much as possible we should bring our sicknesses and injuries to God for healing and wisdom on what to do instead of just assuming that we should run for the doctors first. God often chooses to bless through doctors whether they are Christian or not because He is: Exodus 34:6, "The LORD, the LORD God, merciful and gracious, longsuffering, and abounding in goodness and truth…". He also has told us to bring our problems to Him, 1 Peter 5:7, "casting all your care upon Him, for He cares for you." Therefore we should go to the doctor when necessary under God's direction but we should also seek God's healing.

Healing prayer can be done for ourselves or with other Christians. I have seen many Christians simply accept sickness as a part of life that cannot be avoided. For myself it is mostly a hindrance to being ready for God's will. I have had much success with going to God when I feel sickness coming on and asking Him to remove it so I can be fit to do His will. I think this depends on yielding my life to God, being here not to do my will but the will of the Lord. The Bible does speak of sickness in Christians relating to sin in some circumstances. Speaking about those who don't examine their hearts before taking the Lord's supper it says in 1 Corinthians 11:30, "For this reason many are weak and sick among you, and many sleep." (See the whole passage in 1 Corinthians 11:17-34.) In the book of James we have the Lord's direction for his people who are sick. We should try to practice this when possible helping one another to overcome our sicknesses. James 5:13-16 "Is anyone among you sick? Let him call for the elders of the church, and let them pray over him, anointing him with oil in the name of the Lord. And the prayer of faith will save the sick, and the Lord will raise him up. And if he has committed sins, he will be forgiven. Confess your trespasses to one another, and pray for one another, that you may be healed."

Chapter Seventeen

Concluding the Matter.

Are you feeling overwhelmed yet? How long is this healing and restoring process supposed to take from start to finish anyway? For me it has been a work in progress. I have gained much freedom and am more at peace within myself than I have ever been before. How long has that taken? It has been accomplished in me by God's grace and truth over the course of the last 26 and more years. Thankfully He worked on the bigger problems that were destroying my life first. Each year has held it's own problems or issues or sins that God has called on me to face and work out with Him. Is God done yet? I would never ask God to stop leading me to things that are going to help me to grow spiritually and to become more like Jesus. In my early years I used to work hard at getting God to fix me. Now I have learned that He will bring all these things in their order and in His time as long as I stay willing to do business with Him. I still hold onto Him in prayer for the change once I know what it is supposed to be. And, yes, I still have bad days scattered among the blessed ones. I'm not sure how long it will take for you. That really depends on you being willing and God working out His plan. I do know you will be blessed every time you have a victory with God.

I'm sure that there are other areas of slavery to sin that can be worked out between a person and God. I have written about the ones, which through personal experience, I am the most familiar with. I want to encourage you to want to be free. I know it can look like a long dark tunnel. However, God will give the victory to anyone who is willing to work with Him to break free from slavery to sin. That victory is very sweet and each time a problem is overcome we gain hope as we become more and more free. John 8:36, "Therefore if the Son makes you free, you shall be free indeed." There is nothing too hard for The Lord. He can make a person free regardless of where they have to live or what their opportunities in life end up being, in a ghetto, in a prison cell, in a palace, anywhere. Also look for your God to make opportunities for you. His word states in Ephesians 2:10 that, "we are His workmanship, created in Christ Jesus for good works, which God prepared beforehand that we should walk in them." This verse is truth no matter who you are, where you are, where you have been, or what you have done, as long as you have received Christ and dedicated yourself to walking in Him. The next part of this book will deal directly with this subject.

Part Three

Living a Life of Freedom,

Jesus is the Life!

Chapter Eighteen

Building in the Good.

I have noticed something in my talks with prisoners, which is also true in me and I suspect is true for most of us. We have a tendency towards focusing mainly or only on what is wrong with us. As important as it is to work through and root out the areas of sin we have in our lives it is equally important that we work with God to build the good things of His kingdom into our lives. From our focus verse we know that Jesus is the life, He is life. His words from John 10:10 also tell us so, "I have come that they may have life, and that they may have it more abundantly." It would be wrong to ignore areas of bondage in our soul as we press forward to live for God. It is equally wrong to get so wrapped up in fixing what is wrong with us that we do not 'live' with and for the Lord each day. There will always be times when God is after something big in us that He just wants out of the way. During those times problem solving could become a main focus. But even then we should not forget to live out the life and 'good works' for which we were created in Christ.

Chapter Nineteen

The Good Fruit of God's Holy Spirit.

We spent a lot of time in the last chapter on the bad fruit of sin, trespass, transgression, which grows from the unholy roots of iniquity or wickedness. One of the greatest parts of salvation in Christ is the gift of His Holy Spirit. Acts 2:38-39, "Repent, and let every one of you be baptized in the name of Jesus Christ for the remission of sins; and you shall receive the gift of the Holy Spirit. For the promise is to you and to your children, and to all who are afar off, as many as the Lord our God will call." The Holy Spirit of the Lord becomes God's Holy root in you to bear good fruit for God.

Ephesians 5:8-11 reads, "For you were once darkness, but now you are light in the Lord. Walk as children of light (for the fruit of the Spirit is in all goodness, righteousness, and truth), finding out what is acceptable to the Lord. And have no fellowship with the unfruitful works of darkness, but rather expose them." As Christians, if we have any question about whether we should be involved in something or not we can examine it and ask ourselves if it is part of the goodness, righteousness, and truth of God's Holy Spirit or not. If not then it will not bear good fruit in our lives and we will only be hurt and cause hurt by pursuing it.

In the New Testament book of Galatians Paul teaches us that we now have the Spirit of God but that we still have our own 'flesh', our selfish nature, these two are working against each other within us. Galatians 5:16-18, "I say then: Walk in the Spirit, and you shall not fulfill the lust of the flesh. For the flesh lusts against the Spirit, and the Spirit against the flesh; and these are contrary to one another, so that you do not do the things that you wish. But if you are led by the Spirit, you are not under the law." This is what we should now want as believers and followers of Jesus Christ. We want to walk daily in the Spirit of God who is in us and not by our own flesh or sinful nature. We want to build the things and behaviors into our lives that will bring the life and peace of Jesus Christ, the things that will make us ready as ministers of His grace and truth to others. We want to be led of the Spirit rather than being under the condemnation and judgment of God's law. Paul continues by laying out the things that our lusting 'flesh' desires. If we follow our 'flesh' or selfish nature then these are the things that will end up filling our lives. He then tells us of the nine things that are the fruit of God's Spirit. If we walk in His Spirit these are the things, the fruit, which will end up filling our lives. Notice that, although there are laws of God with judgment against the works of the flesh, he tells us that there are no laws against the fruit of the Spirit. We can have as much of these good things as we desire. Galatians 5:19-26, "Now the works of the flesh are evident, which are: adultery, fornication, uncleanness, lewdness, idolatry, sorcery, hatred, contentions, jealousies, outbursts of wrath, selfish ambitions, dissensions, heresies, envy, murders, drunkenness, revelries, and the like; of which I tell you beforehand, just as I also told you in time past, that those who practice such things will not inherit the kingdom of God. But the fruit of the Spirit is love, joy, peace, longsuffering, kindness, goodness, faithfulness, gentleness, self-control. Against such there is no law. And those who are Christ's have crucified the flesh with its passions and desires. If we live in the Spirit, let us also walk in the Spirit. Let us not become conceited, provoking one another, envying one another."

The fruit of God's Spirit is supposed to grow in every Christian's life. It should be replacing the works of the flesh but it is not automatic. It does not just happen. The truth is we cannot make this fruit to grow in our lives, only God can do that. However, we do have a responsibility to cooperate with God and to work with Him as He works in us to bring this about. Our assurance can come from one of the promises of God found in Philippians 1:6, "being confident of this very thing, that He who has begun a good work in you will complete it until the day of Jesus Christ". Our cooperation with God on this lifelong project of renewal includes at least the following:

1. Spending regular time in God's word and prayer to learn of Him and His truth.
2. Working with God to overcome any known sin or cycle of slavery to sin in our lives.
3. Living for Him daily in the light of the truth we have been given, repenting when we stumble and getting back up and going again as soon as possible.
4. Asking God to work in us to give us victory in overcoming the flesh and to give us the fruit of His Holy Spirit, (Luke 11:13, Matthew 6:13).

(What true-hearted earthly father could resist such cooperation in a son or daughter and yet we serve better than any earthly father, we have the Heavenly Father who is perfect in every way and has our very best in mind.)

The book of James gives us an example of the fruit of the Spirit helping us to overcome the trials which life brings us and not just overcome them but come out of the end a stronger and better person. James 1:2-5, "My brethren, count it all joy when you fall into various trials, knowing that the testing of your faith produces patience. But let patience have its perfect work, that you may be perfect and complete, lacking nothing." The fruit here is a combination of joy and patience. Joy is directly mentioned and the word used in the New Testament for patience in this verse means the same as the word for longsuffering, mentioned as one part of the fruit of the Spirit, but it also adds the idea of joyfulness to the longsuffering. Now, no one likes trials or difficulties in life, but they come whether we like them or not. How will we face them? Will we let them under our skin and into our flesh until they drive us crazy and we explode in anger or swearing? I know that happens to me at times. Or will we face them with the joy and longsuffering of the Spirit? For me I have to connect to the end result. I have to want to be, as it says, 'perfect and entire lacking nothing'. When I want this good quality that God will build in me then I can be more dedicated to joy and 'let' patience have it's perfect work during trials. (Wow, I just wrote this and do I ever need to hear it myself.)

The fruit of the Spirit is love. There are nine parts of the fruit of the Spirit listed in the verses of Galatians we covered above. The word fruit is singular not plural, it is fruit not fruits. Because of this we know that all these nine things are connected to each other. Some believe that since love is listed first that all the other parts are really a part of love. Whether that is true or not, love is the greatest and certainly first part of the fruit of the Spirit. It starts with love, the love of God for us, our love returned to Him. Without love we have nothing. We entered into Christ through understanding our need for salvation. At some point it became clear that, yes, we were sinners and headed for God's judgment or that we were lost and Jesus was holding out a hand of hope to us. So we took that step and received Him. Now we are starting out to live for Him. The truest picture of love, John 15:13 "Greater love has no one than this, than to lay down one's life for his friends", has been shown to us. Jesus Christ the Son of God has laid down His life to save us. The living God has actually counted us as friends. But often, because of our upbringing, we do not really understand what love is.

First of all there are different kinds of love and different ways in which we think about love. Greek is the original language of the New Testament and in Greek there are different words for different kinds of love. There is the Greek word Phileo pronounced fill-lay-o, which means brotherly love like the love between close friends. If any of you are from 'Philly' it is from this word that we get Philadelphia, which means 'the city of brotherly love'. Phileo love is the 'feeling' kind of love from the heart. Jesus said that God the Father loves (Phileo) those who love (Phileo) Jesus, (John 16:27). Another Greek word, not used in the Bible, is Eros, which is the sexual love meant to be between a husband and wife, from this word we get our word erotic which has a somewhat different meaning. Often all we saw of 'love' while growing up was erotic love. Some of you had moms with many men or dads with many women or had rejection from parents and went looking for sexual love to satisfy your need for love. Still another Greek word, Koinonia pronounced coin-o-knee-a, describes fellowship love between those who believe in God together. Our main Greek word for understanding love is agape, pronounced uh-gop-ay taken from the Greek word Agapao pronounced Uh-ga-pay-o. This is the word used as part of the fruit of the Spirit. The concept or idea of Agape love is the main focus of the New Testament because it describes God's love towards us when we don't deserve it. Agape love is love that chooses to love, giving the expressions of love unconditionally and living un-selfishly towards others. Agape love chooses to love even those who do not love in return and cares for people whether they even know about it or not. It is with this agape love that God the Father gave His Son Jesus for us, John 3:16 "For God so loved (Agapao) the world that He gave His only begotten Son, that whoever believes in Him should not perish but have everlasting life." The following points should help us understand the true nature of God's agape love and how it can be built into our lives. I also recommend that you read the small New Testament book of First John, (1 John), most of which is written about this agape love.

In 1 John 4:19 we read that, "We love Him because He first loved us." Our love for God is based on His having loved us first. As Jesus said, "You did not choose Me, but I chose you...", (John 15:16). Because our love for Him flows out of His love for us it is important to understand the nature of His love. We have already seen that God's love for the world moved Him to send Jesus to suffer and become the Savior of the world. Romans 5:6-8 also shows us this love of God bringing it down to the level of the individual sinner, you and me, "For when we were still without strength, in due time Christ died for the ungodly. For scarcely for a righteous man will one die; yet perhaps for a good man someone would even dare to die. But God demonstrates His own love toward us, in that while we were still sinners, Christ died for us." Not after we became good enough, not after we understood His 'religion', not after we did many good works, but while we were still sinners and enemies of the righteous God, He died for us to save us. That is God's choice of unconditional, unselfish, giving, agape love. Why would God do this for us? What is it about God that He would even care about the people living on this small planet in the tiny Milky Way Galaxy off in a corner of the vast universe? John tells us what it is about God that He would give Himself for us and then seek us out to follow Him. In 1 John 4:8 we read, "He who does not love does not know God, for God is love." <u>God is Love.</u> This is probably the most defining statement about God in the whole Bible. It explains a lot of things for me. It is not telling me that God is just some cosmic force known as love that we think about or feel, rather it is talking about the very nature of the person we know as God. Back whenever it was that God decide what kind of person He was going to be I'm so glad that He chose to be a loving, kind, and merciful God. All of the good things I know about God can be summed up in this one thing, that God is love. That is why He would care about us, that is why He would go to the length that He did in saving us through Jesus, because He does love us, it is His very nature, it is the way God is.

Hopefully as Christians, saved through this very love of God, we are growing up in Christ developing a heart that wants to return this same kind of love to our Heavenly Father. How do we do that? How does a child of God show God that we also love Him? In John 14:21-24 Jesus gives us the answer, "'He who has My commandments and keeps them, it is he who loves Me. And he who loves Me will be loved by My Father, and I will love him and manifest Myself to him.' Judas (not Iscariot) said to Him, 'Lord, how is it that You will manifest Yourself to us, and not to the world?' Jesus answered and said to him, 'If anyone loves Me, he will keep My word; and My Father will love him, and We will come to him and make Our home with him. He who does not love Me does not keep My words; and the word which you hear is not Mine but the Father's who sent Me.'" From these verses we can clearly see that returning love to God is done by choosing to keep His word, obeying Him. In fact it not only returns love to God but it brings us closer to God as Jesus said that He and the Father will come to this one who keeps His word and actually make Their home in that person. Jesus said He would 'manifest' Himself to such a person. Manifest means to show or declare Himself. (This connects with the verses just before this in John 14:15-18 where Jesus promises that the Spirit of God will live with us and be in us who are His.) My reaction is Wow! Yes! I want to learn to keep your word more and more if it is going to mean that God is with me. I realize that some of you may find this discouraging. How am I going to do that? How am I going to keep all of the words of Jesus? I've never been able to before! If that is your reaction then I want to encourage you. Remember that part of the 'word' is that when we stumble or fail we can and should repent, seek God's forgiveness, and He will get us back up and going, (1 John 1:9). Remember Philippians1:6, "being confident of this very thing, that He who has begun a good work in you will complete it until the day of Jesus Christ". He would not be working in you if there was nothing that needed work. So be encouraged, continue to follow, it is with our will the we choose God's way and His way will develop the right heart in us for keeping His word.

Now what words do we keep? In what is commonly known as the great commission Jesus commanded His followers to: "Go therefore and make disciples of all the nations, baptizing them in the name of the Father and of the Son and of the Holy Spirit, teaching them to observe all things that I have commanded you; and lo, I am with you always, even to the end of the age", (Matthew 28:19-

20). It is the job of those who are saved to take the truths of the Lord Jesus to others and not only share with them the gospel message of salvation, that they also may become disciples of the Lord, but also teach them to observe or do all the things Jesus has commanded us. They are then to do the same, which is how God's church, his people, grows in numbers and strength. What would be the first of God's commandments we might teach them after someone decides to follow the Lord? In Matthew 22:35-40 we read: "Then one of them, a lawyer, asked Him a question, testing Him, and saying, 'Teacher, which is the great commandment in the law?' Jesus said to him, "'You shall love the LORD your God with all your heart, with all your soul, and with all your mind.' This is the first and great commandment. And the second is like it: 'You shall love your neighbor as yourself.' On these two commandments hang all the Law and the Prophets.'" Jesus quoted to the lawyer two verses from the Old Testament books of the law, love God and love your neighbor. He said that the rest of the commandments hang on those two. Now we have a proper framework for looking at all of God's commandments. If all of the commandments hang on the two that are about love then all of the commandments of God are somehow about love. The Bible can give us the details of how to love God and how to love our neighbor or fellow man through the rest of the commandments. An example of a more detailed commandment that describes 'how' to love our neighbor would be Titus 3:1-2 which says, "to speak evil of no one, to be peaceable, gentle, showing all humility to all men". I hope you are getting the picture. God has chosen to love us and has shown that love to us through salvation in Jesus. We love Him because He first loved us and we want to show Him that we love Him. We show Him that we love Him by keeping His word, His commandments. His word commands us to love God and love your neighbor and gives us further commands that describe 'how' to do so. It is all about agape love, the choice to love unselfishly, which is the greatest of the fruits, which God's Spirit will be working to bring out in you as His child.

Are there any commandments of God in the Bible that we should not try to obey? The answer is yes. In Matthew 5:17-19 Jesus said: "Do not think that I came to destroy the Law or the Prophets. I did not come to destroy but to fulfill. For assuredly, I say to you, till heaven and earth pass away, one jot or one tittle will by no means pass from the law till all is fulfilled. Whoever therefore breaks one of the least of these commandments, and teaches men so, shall be called least in the kingdom of heaven; but whoever does and teaches them, he shall be called great in the kingdom of heaven." When Jesus mentions the law and the prophets He is talking about the Old Testament. The coming of Jesus brought something new from God for man, the words of which we call the New Testament. But here Jesus states that He did not come to destroy the Old Testament but to fulfill it. He says not one jot or tittle will pass from the law till all is fulfilled, jots and tittles were the tiniest markings in the Hebrew alphabet. The Old Testament was written mostly in Hebrew and their lettering could take on a different meaning if the 'jots and tittles' were missing. So Jesus is saying that the whole law of God from the Law and Prophets of the Old Testament still stands until it is fulfilled. So what do I mean when I say that there are some commandments of God we should not try to obey? I mean the ones Jesus has fulfilled. We do not need to try and obey all of the Old Testament commandments about how to offer sacrifices of animals and grain to God. We do not need to try and obey all the ceremonial washings or eating and drinking laws or many of the laws about what is clean and unclean. We do not need to do those things because Jesus is the fulfillment of the sacrificial laws and the laws about what is clean and unclean. In John 1:29, John the Baptist declares of Jesus: "Behold! The Lamb of God who takes away the sin of the world!" Jesus has become God's sacrifice for sin, Jesus has made us clean in God's sight. We can learn much from those parts of the Old Testament but should not try to actually do them.

Before we leave this very important subject of love let's look at what is commonly called the 'love' chapter, 1 Corinthians chapter 13. I will just print the main part of it here without further comment other than to say this is what God's agape love looks like and this is what the love He is calling us to should grow to look like. Some older Bible translations will use the word charity instead of love in these verses but it is still the Greek word agape. 1 Corinthians 13:4-8, "Love suffers long and is kind; love does not envy; love does not parade itself, is not puffed up; does not behave rudely, does not seek its own, is not provoked, thinks no evil; does not rejoice in iniquity, but rejoices in the truth; bears all things, believes all things, hopes all things, endures all things. Love never fails." Verse 13, "And now abide faith, hope, love, these three; but the greatest of these is love."

We have been adopted by God, set free from judgment for our sins, given the promise of eternal life through Jesus Christ our Lord. Given His Holy Spirit to live within us growing us in good fruit and guiding us. Let us grow and learn to serve our God from a loving heart of obedience to His commandments, not because we need to do so for our salvation, we are already saved through the blood of Jesus Christ, but let us do so as our way of loving Him who loved us first.

Chapter Twenty

Learning How to Do Good.

Ephesians 2:8-10 "For by grace you have been saved through faith, and that not of yourselves; it is the gift of God, not of works, lest anyone should boast. For we are His workmanship, created in Christ Jesus for good works, which God prepared beforehand that we should walk in them." These verses bring two important things together in one place. We see the fact that we are saved by grace not by any works that we have done, no one will be able to boast of their works as better or more important. We also see the fact that God created us in Christ for good works, not just any good works but ones that He prepared beforehand that we should walk in them. God not only knows us better than we could imagine, but God has also prepared a plan for you and me complete with the works He wants us to do. In the last section we looked at returning God's love through keeping His commandments. The Bible has many commandments which show God's will for our lives and it also has much to teach us about what is 'good' and what is not.

Many times the society we live in makes up it's own mind about what is 'good', even in our prisons there is an understanding among prisoners about what is OK to do and what is not. As Christians we have to remember that God does not change His word or His standard of what is right and wrong, good and bad, just because man does. For example in our day the world is telling us that sex outside of marriage and even homosexuality are OK. Research has been announced that seems to say that people cannot help being alcoholics or drug addicts. The world has played with the idea that people can't help being criminals because they are 'victims' of bad upbringing and environment. But God's word does not change, what God has said about right and wrong, good and bad remains. Jesus put it like this: "Heaven and earth will pass away, but My words will by no means pass away", (Luke 21:33).

'Good' is often something we need to learn to do and learning to do good is part of God's call to us. In Isaiah 1:16-17 we read: "Wash yourselves, make yourselves clean; Put away the evil of your doings from before My eyes. Cease to do evil, Learn to do good; Seek justice, Rebuke the oppressor; Defend the fatherless, Plead for the widow." An example of Jesus' clear expectation for us to do good is Matthew 25:34-40, "Then the King will say to those on His right hand, 'Come, you blessed of My Father, inherit the kingdom prepared for you from the foundation of the world: for I was hungry and you gave Me food; I was thirsty and you gave Me drink; I was a stranger and you took Me in; I was naked and you clothed Me; I was sick and you visited Me; I was in prison and you came to Me.' Then the righteous will answer Him, saying, 'Lord, when did we see You hungry and feed You, or thirsty and give You drink? When did we see You a stranger and take You in, or naked and clothe

You? Or when did we see You sick, or in prison, and come to You?' And the King will answer and say to them, 'Assuredly, I say to you, inasmuch as you did it to one of the least of these My brethren, you did it to Me.'"

Now let me put this together from what I have stated and quoted above. We were saved by God's grace not by our works, but also created in Christ for good works, which God has planned for us to do. God calls us to stop doing evil and 'learn' to do good. The word of God has many commandments and other things to say and teach about what is good to do and what is not. The examples from Isaiah and Matthew show us that that good works are often if not always connected to something we do for others, defend the fatherless, plead for the widow, care for the hungry, thirsty, naked, visit those sick or in prison. As we have seen before other parts of the word call us to spread the gospel and teach God's truths to others.

Expanding a little more on the idea that God has already planned certain good works for each of us to do I would like to point out that the Bible is God's general will for man, the Holy Spirit of God living within you can tell you God's specific will for you and what God would have you to do. Let me explain. The Bible teaches us that if we see our neighbor in need we should help them and that it does not matter if that neighbor is a friend or an enemy, (Matthew 5:43-48). Now if I see my neighbor struggling with a flat tire I do not need to 'hear' from the Holy Spirit that I should offer to help them, the Bible is already clear about what I should do. On the other hand, as we read earlier, the Bible teaches a lot of good works that will need more direction or definition. Defend the fatherless, plead for the widow, how Lord, what exactly would you have me do to defend them and which ones should I personally help? Visit the sick and prisoner, yes Lord, which hospitals or prisons should I go to and who should

I see there this day? You see there is a need for specific
instructions from God's Holy Spirit. Jesus taught us the
role of the Holy Spirit in John 14:26, "But the Helper, the
Holy Spirit, whom the Father will send in My name, He
will teach you all things, and bring to your remembrance
all things that I said to you." Further in the same book
of John 16:13-14 "However, when He, the Spirit of truth,
has come, He will guide you into all truth; for He will not
speak on His own authority, but whatever He hears He
will speak; and He will tell you things to come. He will
glorify Me, for He will take of what is Mine and declare
it to you." So we do have everything we need to 'learn
to do good', we have the Bible as our guidebook and the
Holy Spirit of God to teach us all things that we need to
know about exactly what we should do, what God's plan
of good works is for us.

When we first come to Christ and before we have
spent much time getting to know God, learning His
word, learning how to pray and listen in prayer, it can
be difficult to 'hear' what the Holy Spirit would have
us do. Growing in hearing the Holy Spirit comes with
time, with obedience in doing what we already know,
and patience. It is like learning to speak and hear a new
language. If you live in a noisy city and then go out into
the country you will not hear all of the quiet country
noises right away. A person who has lived in the country
for a while has more sensitive hearing for the still small
noises of the country. This is because our minds block
out what we think of as useless background noise. We
have to develop the patience and sensitivity to hear the
Lord's voice after years of ignoring it. You also need to
understand that there is a battle that goes on inside of us
between our flesh, our selfish nature, and the Holy Spirit.
We have already talked about this earlier. The important
thing to know here, from the book of John quoted above,

is that the Holy Spirit is taking what belongs to Jesus and making it known or declaring it to you. Therefore what He will declare to you will not be in agreement with your own selfishness, which may try to get in the way, and it will never disagree with the written word of God, the Bible. For example, if you are seeking to know something from God in prayer for a selfish reason then you may hear something but it will be your flesh and not God's Spirit, (1 John 4:1, James 4:1-10). In order to hear from the Lord's Spirit we have to let God drive the car. Our job is to sit back, put the gear in neutral so the car is not wanting to go forward or in reverse, and then take our hands off of the steering wheel and let the Lord do the driving. Set aside where we want to go and be willing to go where He wants to go. This way the direction we take will be from God and not from us.

When I was just beginning to follow the Lord I had no idea or expectation that He would actually speak to me in my spirit. I was busy studying the Bible, serving in the church, sharing the faith when I could, and I had started to pray every day. My prayers were just a list of all the people I wanted the Lord to bless or work in and the things I needed. I prayed that way for the better part of a year. One morning, as I was on my knees praying, the Lord spoke to me. I did not hear a voice with my ears but it came clear in my spirit. I was surprised so I listened again and again I heard Him say to me, "I anoint you to preach my word". I was excited, but then I began to doubt. I searched the Bible to see if we are supposed to be 'hearing' from God and I found the same verses that I have already shared with you above. I also saw many examples of God speaking and making His will known to people of the past in the Bible and so I believed. Because of that word I began to learn to preach, first in church, then on the mission field, and so on. That being just one example, I slowly developed and grew in hearing from the Lord in prayer rather than just talking at Him. There were some hard lessons along the way. I learned from failures that I must approach God for His plan and not bring a plan of my own along. But I also learned that I could trust God in what I heard from Him, it would be the right thing to do and I could step out in faith on it. Over the years I have come to a place where I will not make daily life decisions about what I will or won't do without asking God and waiting on Him to hear what He wants. I don't usually ask Him about small stuff like what I should have for breakfast or what to wear that day, but sometimes I do. Whether it is about ministry, where to live, where to work, what to do with my family, how to do a specific job or task, I am much better off in His hands and under the direction of the Holy Spirit. As the Bible says, "Or do you not know that your body is the temple of the Holy Spirit who is in you, whom you have from God, and you are not your own? For you were bought at a price; therefore glorify God in your body and in your spirit, which are God's", (1 Corinthians 6:19-20).

Lastly let me add that as individuals we often think that everything is about us. Feed the hungry, visit the sick, and spread the gospel, to the whole world? Yes to the whole world, but how we do this is important to notice. God does not expect you personally to do all of this work. That is why there are other Christians and God is raising up more of us each day. Together we are to reach and serve the whole world in His name. If I do the things that God calls me to do and you do the things that God calls you to do then together the job will get done. There will be times He has something for me to do alone that no one can do except me because He made me in Christ for that job. There will be other times when God has me work together with other Christians to do a job. I look up on Friday nights at the tiers, five stories high, 50 cells long, and I know I cannot visit all of the prisoners even if I come for a year, that is a job to big for one person. God knows this and so He has called other men to minister at this prison and get the job done together. We are often use to being loners but in Christ we are part of a larger family. If my brothers and sisters in Christ are on the mission field or working in ministry or in the church were God called them to be and if I am doing the same then 'we' are in ministry, on the mission field, etc. for Jesus Christ. Wherever they are Christ is and I am in Christ together with them. Romans 12:4-8 "For as we have many members in one body, but all the members do not have the same function, so we, being many, are one body in Christ, and individually members of one another. Having then gifts differing according to the grace that is given to us, let us use them: if prophecy, let us prophesy in proportion to our faith; or ministry, let us use it in our ministering; he who teaches, in teaching; he who exhorts, in exhortation; he who gives, with liberality; he who leads, with diligence; he who shows mercy, with cheerfulness."

Chapter Twenty-One

The Importance of Knowing God.

In all that we have covered so far regarding salvation, freedom from slavery to sin, and service to God, I want to make sure to be very clear about the importance of you and I knowing God personally. That is to say, knowing Him person to person. This is an area that can be hard for many of us because we were never close to anyone or never let anyone get very close to us. We may never have experienced a father who knew us and wanted us to know him. Some of our fathers were pretty rough. We may not have had deep friendships where we could be open and real with the other person without getting a negative reaction from them or being put off by them. It is important to understand that, even if we never had them before, God did design us to have close relationships with Himself and others. In God our Heavenly Father we will find that true Father who does know everything there is to know about us, the good and the bad, and yet He loves us with His agape love and wants us to become close to Him and know Him. In Jesus we do find that true friend.

In Proverbs 18:24 the Bible gives us a hint about what Jesus' friendship will be like, "A man who has friends must himself be friendly, But there is a friend who sticks closer than a brother." Jesus is the friend who will stick closer than a brother, a friend who understands us, who knows us, who is not afraid to tell us the truth about ourselves. He is a friend who we can be open and honest with and bring our deepest problems and fears to Him for help. It is an awesome thing that the living God, whom we do need to respect and are called to obey, desires that we come to know Him, sharing both love and friendship with Him.

We know that: "...the wages of sin is death, but the gift of God is eternal life in Christ Jesus our Lord", (Romans 6:23). What is eternal life? We often think of it as everlasting life, we shall be with God and we shall never die. The Bible describes the beauty of eternal life with God, (see Revelation chapters 21 and 22), in Revelation 21:3-5 we read: "And I heard a loud voice from heaven saying, 'Behold, the tabernacle of God is with men, and He will dwell with them, and they shall be His people. God Himself will be with them and be their God. And God will wipe away every tear from their eyes; there shall be no more death, nor sorrow, nor crying. There shall be no more pain, for the former things have passed away.' Then He who sat on the throne said, 'Behold, I make all things new.'" These things are true and as Christians we look forward to them after our life of service is over and when our Lord Jesus returns. But in that heaven, in that place with no tears, no pain, will we be close to God or will He be a distant person over there on the throne that you would be afraid to approach? Jesus taught us that the very heart of the eternal life He came to bring us is a close relationship with He and Father God. On the night before He died we hear the beginning of Jesus prayer, John 17:1-

3, "Jesus spoke these words, lifted up His eyes to heaven, and said: 'Father, the hour has come. Glorify Your Son, that Your Son also may glorify You, as You have given Him authority over all flesh, that He should give eternal life to as many as You have given Him. And this is eternal life, that they may know You, the only true God, and Jesus Christ whom You have sent.'" From this we know that it is the prayer of Jesus and God's intention that we 'know' Him. This is eternal life, to know God. Knowing God is the very thing that eternal life is all about.

Jeremiah 9:23-24, "Thus says the LORD: 'Let not the wise man glory in his wisdom, let not the mighty man glory in his might, nor let the rich man glory in his riches; but let him who glories glory in this, that he understands and knows Me, that I am the LORD, exercising lovingkindness, judgment, and righteousness in the earth. For in these I delight,' says the LORD."

Jesus said in John 10:14, "I am the good shepherd; and I know My sheep, and am known by My own." We are the sheep of the Lord, His flock, His people. It is important that we understand that we are to come to know Him better and better purely for the sake of a loving relationship between our God and us as He intended it to be. It is out of such a relationship that we end up understanding who we are as individuals, that we receive His comfort during our troubles, that we develop proper desires to return love to our God through service and obedience. As we go on in prayer, in the word, in service and obedience we grow as individuals, learning more of the heart of God and the mind of God towards ourselves and towards our fellow man. James put it like this: James 4:7-8 "Draw near to God and He will draw near to you."

Chapter Twenty-Two

A New Commandment.

Jesus' mission of salvation and restoration of individuals to God broke through all of man's barriers of prejudice. Salvation was not just for the Jews or any other group or groups of people. This grace of God extended through Jesus is offered to all mankind regardless of race, gender, nation, previous religion, or anything else. The Bible shows us the final picture of the nations of those who are saved in Revelation 7:9-10, "After these things I looked, and behold, a great multitude which no one could number, of all nations, tribes, peoples, and tongues, standing before the throne and before the Lamb, clothed with white robes, with palm branches in their hands, and crying out with a loud voice, saying, 'Salvation belongs to our God who sits on the throne, and to the Lamb!'" (Note: Jesus is the 'lamb of God', see John 1:29.)

The ridiculous prejudices of man have no place in the kingdom of God. It was always God's intent to bring all of His own back together in Christ as brothers and sisters of the same family. In order to do this Jesus started the

'Church'. The beginning of the Church was a gathering of 12 men who Jesus called to follow Him. This grew into a larger group of men and women. At one time in the book of Luke we see Jesus sending out 70 in groups of two to preach and heal in every town He planned to visit. Over 500 believers saw Jesus after He had risen from the dead, (1 Corinthians 15:3-8). Thousands were added to the church at the day of Pentecost. Acts 2:47, "And the Lord added to the church daily those who were being saved." As we read the book of Acts we see that the Church expanded from Jerusalem to the Jews in Judea, then to the Samaritans in Samaria, then it covered the entire Roman world and beyond. Three hundred years later, after many harsh Roman persecutions in which thousands of Christians were killed, the Church was still going strong. At this time in history, the Roman Emperor Constantine and his mother became Christians and made Christianity the official religion of the Roman Empire and the Roman persecutions stopped. From that time to this the Church has grown mightily in the entire world through missionary and witnessing activity of one kind or another. Over these almost two thousand years there have been people and so called 'Christian' churches that have done much evil in the name of the Lord and led many others astray from God. But those of every race and people who have been saved and do know and follow the Lord Jesus have always continued on in His ways throughout history. The Church is far from just being a building here or there, rather than buildings it is God's people who are His Church, (1 Peter 2:5).

So those who believe are very special to the Lord, we are His Church and He wants us to recognize each other as equals and as brothers and sisters. To this end Jesus has given us a new commandment that we may know how to live towards those who are also in Christ. John 13:34-

35, "A new commandment I give to you, that you love one another; as I have loved you, that you also love one another. By this all will know that you are My disciples, if you have love for one another." When Christians of all kinds love one another the world can then see that we belong to Christ. This honors our Lord and provides a setting in which the works of the Lord can thrive. Where you find Christians arguing over minor points of the Bible, or treating each other with disrespect in their families or churches, divided or even hating one another, then the world that needs salvation looks on and wonders how there could be a God. These divisions among us do not honor God and have no place in the Kingdom of Heaven. If a person has come to God in repentance, has believed in God's Son Jesus Christ and received Him as their Savior and Lord, and they are making an honest attempt to follow Him rather than making excuses for their sins, then that person is living as your brother or sister in Christ. They deserve to be treated as brother or sister even if the two of you don't agree about every other teaching of the Bible. (Even if they don't understand that they are to treat you as brother or sister.) Again, if another Christian lives or works where you do, or is a member of your family and yet you see some fault in them that they don't understand or are not facing up to, then they still deserve to be treated with respect and kindness. We have to trust God that through patient sharing of the truth with one another the Holy Spirit will lead those of us who are saved into all truth, (see John 16:13 and 2 Timothy 2:24-26).

To go along with Jesus' new commandment, that Disciples of Christ should 'love one another', there are many verses in the rest of the New Testament that use the words 'one another'. These other verses show us 'how' to love one another. I am going to list a number of them but before I do let me say, for the sake of those of us who are used to being independent loners, that no man is an island. There will never be a time when we don't need one another for fellowship or for counsel and confirmation about the heavier decisions in life or for comfort and friendship during the tough times. Christians balance one another. Common mistakes about following God are made when we bypass the balance that other believers bring to us. Those other believers may be the saints who wrote the Bible or they may be the fellow believers who you get to see every day and maybe even go to church services or Bible studies with. God's intention is that the different members of His Church strengthen, encourage, and help one another.

Romans 12:10, "Be kindly affectionate to *one another* with brotherly love, in honor giving preference to *one another*".

Romans 12:16, "Be of the same mind toward *one another*. Do not set your mind on high things, but associate with the humble. Do not be wise in your own opinion."

Romans 13:8, "Owe no one anything except to love *one another*, for he who loves another has fulfilled the law."

Romans 14:13, "Therefore let us not judge *one another* anymore, but rather resolve this, not to put a stumbling block or a cause to fall in our brother's way."

Romans 14:19, "Therefore let us pursue the things which make for peace and the things by which *one* may edify *another*."

Romans 15:7, "Therefore receive *one another*, just as Christ also received us, to the glory of God."

1 Corinthians 12:25, "that there should be no schism in the body, but that the members should have the same care for *one another*."

Galatians 5:13, "For you, brethren, have been called to liberty; only do not use liberty as an opportunity for the flesh, but through love serve *one another*."

Galatians 5:15, "But if you bite and devour *one another*, beware lest you be consumed by *one another!*

Galatians 5:26, "Let us not become conceited, provoking *one another*, envying *one another*."

Galatians 6:2, "Bear *one another's* burdens, and so fulfill the law of Christ."

Ephesians 4:2, "with all lowliness and gentleness, with longsuffering, bearing with *one another* in love".

Ephesians 4:25, "Therefore, putting away lying, 'Let each one of you speak truth with his neighbor,' for we are members of *one another*."

Ephesians 4:32, "And be kind to *one another*, tenderhearted, forgiving *one another*, just as God in Christ forgave you."

Colossians 3:13, "bearing with *one another*, and forgiving *one another*, if anyone has a complaint against another; even as Christ forgave you, so you also must do."

James 4:11, "Do not speak evil of *one another*, brethren. He who speaks evil of a brother and judges his brother, speaks evil of the law and judges the law. But if you judge the law, you are not a doer of the law but a judge."

James 5:16, "Confess your trespasses to *one another*, and pray for *one another*, that you may be healed. The effective, fervent prayer of a righteous man avails much."

1 Peter 1:22, "Since you have purified your souls in obeying the truth through the Spirit in sincere love of the brethren, love *one another* fervently with a pure heart".

1 Peter 3:8-9, "Finally, all of you be of one mind, having compassion for *one another*; love as brothers, be tenderhearted, be courteous; not returning evil for evil or reviling for reviling, but on the contrary blessing, knowing that you were called to this, that you may inherit a blessing."

1 Peter 4:8-9, "And above all things have fervent love for *one another,* for 'love will cover a multitude of sins.' Be hospitable to *one another* without grumbling."

I John 3:23, "And this is His commandment: that we should believe on the name of His Son Jesus Christ and love *one another,* as He gave us commandment."

Chapter Twenty-Three

Spiritual Gifts.

The New Testament clearly pictures the Church as being the 'body' of Christ on this earth, with Jesus being the head. I am not going to copy out the main verses here, you can read them in Romans 12:3-51, Corinthians 12:12-27, and Colossians 1:18. These verses further confirm that we are members one of another and that we need each other. We are all created with differences and have different gifts and abilities from God, which He intends to be used in working together to strengthen each other and reach the world for Him. It is important that we do not fall into the trap of comparing ourselves to one another but rather that we learn from God the gifts and abilities that He has specially appointed for each of us. Then, as Peter said in 1 Peter 4:10, "As each one has received a gift, minister it to one another, as good stewards of the manifold grace of God."

We have probably all seen Christians or so called Christians who are immature and are using or trying to use spiritual gifts for their own glory. Focusing on us is one of the main natural tendencies of our fallen sinful nature. Spiritual gifting from God is not given for us to be glorified and admired by others but for us to serve others as Christ served us. For us to operate fully in our spiritual gifting we must determine to grow and mature in humility as Christ was humble. There have been many books written about the gifts of the Spirit, so I will point out just a few necessary things.

The gifts that I am talking about are spiritual gifts. Playing the guitar, fixing cars, or other things we may be able to do to help others are abilities that are learned rather than spiritual gifts. Some people may be better at one or more abilities than others but we are all able to learn different abilities and then use them for good as the Lord leads us. Gifting, in the sense that the Bible is talking about, is of the Holy Spirit and is given to us by God rather than just learned. A Christian should seek God to understand their gifting and then grow in maturity in the use of the same gifts. It is this gifting of the Holy Spirit that helps to define how we fit into the body of Christ, His Church, as functional members. A person with the spiritual gift of evangelism will be used of God to win other people to Jesus through some form of direct contact ministry. That same person may use many abilities like fixing cars for people or playing music or speaking to do the work of evangelism. But it is through the gifting of evangelism that the Spirit of the Lord will work through that person to draw people into His kingdom.

Main lists of the gifts of the Spirit are found in four places in the New Testament and there seems to be a different focus for each list. Prophecy, Ministry, Teaching, Exhortation, Giving, Leading, and Mercy are listed in Romans 12:6-8 and seem to describe the continuous or ongoing ministry or motivation of a person. Word of Wisdom, Word of Knowledge, Faith, Healings, Miracles,

Prophecy, Discerning of spirits, Tongues, Interpretation of Tongues are listed in 1 Corinthians 12:1-11 and seem to be gifts for specific circumstances like when a word is needed or when a healing is needed. In 1 Corinthians 12:28 we see another list that could be a mix of ongoing ministry and individual events, Apostle, Prophet, Teacher, Miracles, Gifts of Healing, Helps, Administration, Varieties of Tongues. In Ephesians 4:11-16 we have a list that is clearly of leadership gifts for building up the body of Christ, Apostles, Prophets, Evangelists, Pastors and Teachers. In my own experience it took time for me to learn my gifting and I am still maturing in how to walk in these things as God directs. God has used me in some healings, I know that I have the gift of Teaching and on some occasions God has given me prophecy or words of knowledge for other people. I do a lot of administration at work but I am not sure if that is a spiritual gift or an ability through which the gift of teaching is then used. As we all learn how the Lord has gifted each of us and as we mature in walking out those gifts then the body of Christ, the Church, will grow as it was intended to do and ministry towards the lost will happen. In seeking to build into our lives the good things of Jesus Christ let us seek God for our gifting and how to use it for His glory. When you think that the Lord is leading you in one of the gifts then I encourage you to take the time to study that gift in the Bible. Which Bible characters had this same gift? How did it operate in their lives? What did God do with them?

One caution needs to be added about spiritual gifts in the same way as it was added by the Apostle Paul, 1 Corinthians 12:31, "But earnestly desire the best gifts. And yet I show you a more excellent way." The more excellent way he mentions is found in the very next chapter, 1 Corinthians 13, which we reviewed as the 'love' chapter.

Earnestly desire the best gifts but whatever God gives you to enable you for ministry it is nothing if you do not have love. Loving people will always be more important than having spiritual gifts.

Chapter Twenty-Four

Living in Partnership with God.

Partnership with God may have a strange sound to it, after all He is the Lord and we are His servants. It is God who makes the rules and commandments and it is for us to obey them. This is very true so what kind of servant will I strive to be for the Lord? Will I be a servant who is just glad he got in the door and will do the minimum, do nothing if I think God is not looking? (See Matthew 24:48) Will I be a servant who knows that what the Master wants is important but really doesn't want to do it and so does it grudgingly or because I feel I have to do it? (See 2 Corinthians 9:7) Or, will I be a servant who is actually more of a friend to his Master? Such a servant knows the Lord's business and why He wants what He does. Such a servant sees their self as part of God's unfolding plan to overcome the evil which man has invited into the world and go with Jesus to 'seek and to save that which was lost', (Luke 19:10). Such a servant will learn not to see people as enemies but rather as those who are in need of God. (See 2 Timothy 2:24-26)

None of us start out in the Lord as this mature servant of God but it should be our goal. Many of us have known the truth but been lazy about it. Many times we have done what God wants but not in a right spirit. Some of us need to spend more time in the Bible, in prayer, in getting to really know God so that we can understand His business and why He wants what He does. My main purpose in the rest of this chapter is to take us through some portions of the Bible helping set our minds and hearts towards becoming this true servant, a partner with God in His business. For this servant of God there will be no greater joy than at the end of life, on entering God's presence, if I would hear the Lord say the words of Matthew 25:21, "Well done, good and faithful servant; you were faithful over a few things, I will make you ruler over many things. Enter into the joy of your lord".

Titus 2:11-14, "For the grace of God that brings salvation has appeared to all men, teaching us that, denying ungodliness and worldly lusts, we should live soberly, righteously, and godly in the present age, looking for the blessed hope and glorious appearing of our great God and Savior Jesus Christ, who gave Himself for us, that He might redeem us from every lawless deed and purify for Himself His own special people, zealous for good works." These very powerful verses can be our starting point for setting our hearts and minds towards becoming true servants of God. His salvation has appeared and has something to teach us. It teaches that our part or partnership with God is to deny ungodliness and worldly lust, live soberly, righteously, and godly in the present age (meaning today). As we do so we open ourselves up to God and give Him the opportunity to work in and through our lives. It is also our part to look for the appearing, the 2nd coming, of Jesus. Looking forward to Jesus' return and the final establishment of righteousness over all evil is a source of great encouragement in our service towards God. Because even though today's individual battles may be difficult we know that in the end there is no question about who wins the war. God's part of this partnership is to redeem us from every lawless deed and purify us for Himself. We are special to God, you and I are special to God. Father God sent His own Son into the world to suffer and endure the punishment of death for our sins so that we can be redeemed, bought back from sin, and become His very own people, (see 2 Corinthians 5:21). A lawless deed is one done from a heart of lawlessness or iniquity. In part two we covered many of the ways that iniquity can be overcome in us that we might be purified. Having saved us Jesus now desires to purify us as 'special' a treasure of His very own. The polish of this treasure is a zeal for good works, a desire for the works God created us for, a desire to walk in partnership with Him to bring His light into this world.

John 15:1-11, "I am the true vine, and My Father is the vinedresser. Every branch in Me that does not bear fruit He takes away; and every branch that bears fruit He prunes, that it may bear more fruit. You are already clean because of the word which I have spoken to you. Abide in Me, and I in you. As the branch cannot bear fruit of itself, unless it abides in the vine, neither can you, unless you abide in Me. I am the vine, you are the branches. He who abides in Me, and I in him, bears much fruit; for without Me you can do nothing. If anyone does not abide in Me, he is cast out as a branch and is withered; and they gather them and throw them into the fire, and they are burned. If you abide in Me, and My words abide in you, you will ask what you desire, and it shall be done for you. By this My Father is glorified, that you bear much fruit; so you will be My disciples. As the Father loved

Me, I also have loved you; abide in My love. If you keep
My commandments, you will abide in My love, just as I
have kept My Father's commandments and abide in His
love. These things I have spoken to you, that My joy may
remain in you, and that your joy may be full."

As followers of Christ we are not the branches that
bear no fruit or that do not abide, meaning to remain,
in the love of Jesus. Those that are taken away, those
that are cast out and burned are the ones who hear the
word gladly but have no root in them and fall away
when following becomes hard or persecution comes, (see
Matthew 13:20-21). This does not include backsliders who
desire to return to the Lord. If a person will return and
be an honest follower of Jesus then their backsliding is
forgiven. God already knew it was going to happen and
they are to be accepted among us as brothers and sisters
in the Lord. Now let's learn a few lessons of partnership
with God from the verses of John 15 above. First, He is the
vine and we are branches, He has made us clean but we
cannot bear fruit by ourselves. A branch only bears fruit
as long as it remains connected to the vine. By ourselves
we can do nothing. Second, Jesus intends that we bear
'much' fruit bringing glory to God the Father. We bear
this fruit through abiding or remaining in Him, in His
love. As it says, if we keep His commandments we will
abide or remain in His love. If we abide in Him and His
words abide in us then we will ask and it will be done
and the Father will be glorified. We will know better than
to ask selfishly when we are in Him and His words in us.
Lastly, Jesus is telling us these things that we may know
Joy in this life-long partnership of being His fruit bearing
branches, of bringing glory to our Heavenly Father.

Jesus said in Luke 11:23, "He who is not with Me
is against Me, and he who does not gather with Me
scatters." We are intended to be co-workers with Christ in

the business of His kingdom, the business of 'gathering' those who will believe and helping them to also follow Him. In fact if we are not learning to be partners with God then what we do with our lives has a negative affect of 'scattering' other people. Others who do not know the Lord actually do look at those of us who say we are Christians. If they see that we do not take His word seriously then they are not likely to do so either. It is important that we do not wait to share what we know in the Lord just because we do not feel we are very good at it or very mature. It is also important that we are honest with people who we share the Lord with, so that they see true humility in us, that we are growing in the Lord changing our old ways and learning new ones with His help. If they come to Jesus for salvation they will also need to grow up in Him. By being honest about what is happening in us we give glory to God and give them a true picture of salvation and life in Christ.

2 Corinthians 5:18-21, "Now all things are of God, who has reconciled us to Himself through Jesus Christ, and has given us the ministry of reconciliation, that is, that God was in Christ reconciling the world to Himself, not imputing their trespasses to them, and has committed to us the word of reconciliation. Now then, we are ambassadors for Christ, as though God were pleading through us: we implore you on Christ's behalf, be reconciled to God. For He made Him who knew no sin to be sin for us, that we might become the righteousness of God in Him." We are ambassadors for Christ. The nations of the world chose only the best and brightest to be their ambassadors and represent them. The Lord chooses all of His children, you and I and every one of us because He is showing the world what His work can be in the hearts and lives of real people. He is calling them to repentance and salvation

and godliness through those who have repented are saved and are becoming godly.

Christian maturity and growth in Christ-likeness come from acting on God's word not just reading or hearing it only. James 1:22, "But be doers of the word, and not hearers only, deceiving yourselves." God's partners are active in God's business and know Him through obedience; they don't just talk about God's business. Matthew 7:21-27 reads: "Not everyone who says to Me, 'Lord, Lord,' shall enter the kingdom of heaven, but he who does the will of My Father in heaven. Many will say to Me in that day, 'Lord, Lord, have we not prophesied in Your name, cast out demons in Your name, and done many wonders in Your name?' And then I will declare to them, 'I never knew you; depart from Me, you who practice lawlessness!' Therefore whoever hears these sayings of Mine, and does them, I will liken him to a wise man who built his house on the rock: and the rain descended, the floods came, and the winds blew and beat on that house; and it did not fall, for it was founded on the rock. Now everyone who hears these sayings of Mine, and does not do them, will be like a foolish man who built his house on the sand: and the rain descended, the floods came, and the winds blew and beat on that house; and it fell. And great was its fall."

2 Peter 3:9-14, "The Lord is not slack concerning His promise, as some count slackness, but is longsuffering toward us, not willing that any should perish but that all should come to repentance. But the day of the Lord will come as a thief in the night, in which the heavens will pass away with a great noise, and the elements will melt with fervent heat; both the earth and the works that are in it will be burned up. Therefore, since all these things will be dissolved, what manner of persons ought you to be in holy conduct and godliness, looking for and hastening the coming of the day of God, because of which the

heavens will be dissolved, being on fire, and the elements will melt with fervent heat? Nevertheless we, according to His promise, look for new heavens and a new earth in which righteousness dwells. Therefore, beloved, looking forward to these things, be diligent to be found by Him in peace, without spot and blameless; and account that the longsuffering of our Lord is salvation". One of the things helping us as believers to keep our focus on partnership with God is the knowledge that mankind and the world are headed towards a final confrontation with the creator of the universe. Sin will not be allowed to continue forever. At present our God is being very longsuffering 'not willing that any should perish but that all should come to repentance'. Jesus is coming back soon to restore all things, maybe in our lifetime. Because of this Peter asks us 'what manner of persons ought you to be in holy conduct and godliness'? Whether we are still living on earth when Jesus returns or when we come to the end of this earthly life we want to be found in Him, living in His peace and busy with the works He has appointed for us. In Matthew 24:45-47 we read, "Who then is a faithful and wise servant, whom his master made ruler over his household, to give them food in due season? Blessed is that servant whom his master, when he comes, will find so doing. Assuredly, I say to you that he will make him ruler over all his goods."

From the teaching of the New Testament we can understand that there were a number of things that distracted believers from focusing on partnership with God. At times we see the early followers of Jesus arguing about who would be greatest among them. Jesus had to teach his first followers not to seek greatness for themselves and that God's leaders are to be servants of the people. Matthew 20:25-28, "But Jesus called them to Himself and said, 'You know that the rulers of the

Gentiles lord it over them, and those who are great exercise authority over them. Yet it shall not be so among you; but whoever desires to become great among you, let him be your servant. And whoever desires to be first among you, let him be your slave-- just as the Son of Man did not come to be served, but to serve, and to give His life a ransom for many.'"

Another great distraction for many Christians is covetousness. Covetousness means wanting something that God has chosen not to give to you. The tenth commandment from the law of Moses is about covetousness, Exodus 20:17, "You shall not covet your neighbor's house; you shall not covet your neighbor's wife, nor his male servant, nor his female servant, nor his ox, nor his donkey, nor anything that is your neighbor's." Today it would probably be car or truck rather than ox or donkey but the idea is the same, God gave it to someone else, it is not yours. God has given us the treasure of His presence and He has promised to give us everything we need in order to live. If we find ourselves focusing on things we have not been given rather than on God the giver of all things then we need to repent of that. The love of money and the love of things has been the downfall of many Christians. God's path is contentment with what He has given us and this is centered in faith and trust in God. Paul was careful to teach this to his disciple Timothy, in 1 Timothy 6:6-10 we read: "Now godliness with contentment is great gain. For we brought nothing into this world, and it is certain we can carry nothing out. And having food and clothing, with these we shall be content. But those who desire to be rich fall into temptation and a snare, and into many foolish and harmful lusts which drown men in destruction and perdition. For the love of money is a root of all kinds of evil, for which some have strayed from the faith in their greediness, and pierced themselves through with many sorrows." It is not that God plans to give every Christian little or nothing, maybe He will and maybe He won't, rather our focus and joy is to be in God not in desiring what we have not been given. The Lord will put His desires, zeal for good works, into our hearts for how we are to serve Him and what kind of life and service it will be and then He will provide as needed for that service. In everything God remains the Christian's treasure, our portion and cup in this world. Hebrews 13:5-6, "Let your conduct be without covetousness; be content with such things as you have. For He Himself has said, 'I will never leave you nor forsake you.' So we may boldly say: 'The LORD is my helper; I will not fear. What can man do to me?'"

John 14:1-6, "'Let not your heart be troubled; you believe in God, believe also in Me. In My Father's house are many mansions; if it were not so, I would have told you. I go to prepare a place for you. And if I go and prepare a place for you, I will come again and receive you to Myself; that where I am, there you may be also. And where I go you know, and the way you know.' Thomas said to Him, 'Lord, we do not know where You are going, and how can we know the way?' Jesus said to him, 'I am the way, the truth, and the life. No one comes to the Father except through Me.'"

I want to encourage you as a Christian to begin to see yourself as a partner with God in His business. His business is our business, it is the most important thing happening on our planet in our time. I know that it is hard to see ourselves as that close or of that much value to God, but we are. A lot of this will come together as we continue to follow, as we work with God to break out of our old cycles of slavery to sin, as we draw close to God and He draws close to us.

Conclusion

It is my personal hope and prayer that you have been and will be greatly blessed by what is shared in this book. My intention has been to bring forth a deeper understanding of God's word the Bible, which can help us to overcome in difficult areas of our lives and in growing into the fullness of Jesus. Jesus Christ is the Way, the Truth, and the Life. I encourage you to follow Him as an over-comer by the strength He will provide (Philippians 4:13), believe His words of truth to light your way (Psalm 119:105), fully embrace the life He has given us in Himself (1 Timothy 6:12).

You can break free from sinful behavior and the cycle of slavery to sin. You do not need to continue to be oppressed and held back in life by bondage to sin but you cannot do it by yourself. No human plan is going to set you free but the Son of God can and will as you cooperate with God's plan for you. The children of Judah were in prison and slavery because they had sinned, they had turned from their God and spent their lives practicing idolatry and all forms of evil. In Jeremiah 29:11-14 we read of God's plan for their restoration: "For I know the thoughts that I think toward you, says the LORD, thoughts of peace and not of evil, to give you a future and a hope. Then you will call upon Me and go and pray to Me, and I will listen to you. And you will seek Me and find Me, when you search for Me with all your heart. I will be found by you, says the LORD, and I will bring you back from your captivity; I will gather you from all the nations and from all the places where I have driven you, says the LORD, and I will bring you to the place from which I cause you to be carried away captive." If you are presently in prison, or just in difficult situations, I do not know what the circumstances of your sentence or situation may be or if it is God's plan to bring you out sooner or ever during your time on this earth. I do know that most of you will get out at some point, some sooner than others. Regardless of how your sentence or situation goes, whether you are in or out, God has His thoughts and plan for you, which can set your soul free from slavery to sin and bring your soul back from where it has been lead captive. God can heal you to the point where you have peace with Him and can lead a life that communicates love with God and your fellow man. It is not God's plan for you to keep returning to prison every time you get out and it is not God's plan for you to live a bitter sin filled life while you are in prison. It is not God's plan for you to keep returning to addictions, self abuse, or the abuse of others. It is God's plan to seal you for eternal life through the Blood of His Son Jesus, for you to come to know Him and become free in Him.

Father God I pray for these my readers, that You will open the eyes and ears of their spirit and give them hearts of understanding in the fullness of all You have provided for us in Jesus Christ. May they be strengthened in Your might by Your Spirit. Deliver them from the evil one and from the sin that so easily besets us. Give them the living hope that is found in Jesus Christ our Lord, In Jesus name I ask it and pray, Amen.

Colossians 1:9-14

"For this reason we also, since the day we heard it, do not cease to pray for you, and to ask that you may be filled with the knowledge of His will in all wisdom and spiritual understanding; that you may have a walk worthy of the Lord, fully pleasing Him, being fruitful in every good work and increasing in the knowledge of God; strengthened with all might, according to His glorious power, for all patience and longsuffering with joy; giving thanks to the Father who has qualified us to be partakers of the inheritance of the saints in the light. He has delivered us from the power of darkness and conveyed us into the kingdom of the Son of His love, in whom we have redemption through His blood, the forgiveness of sins."

Philippians 1:9-11

"And this I pray, that your love may abound still more and more in knowledge and all discernment, that you may approve the things that are excellent, that you may be sincere and without offense till the day of Christ, being filled with the fruits of righteousness which are by Jesus Christ, to the glory and praise of God."

The End, (A New Beginning.)

LaVergne, TN USA
09 January 2011
211689LV00001B/173/A